MAN'S GREATEST FRUSTRATION:

NOT UNDERSTANDING HIS WIFE

Adriana Calabria

A BOOK FOR MEN THAT EVERY WOMAN MUST READ

COMMENTS ABOUT

Man's greatest frustration

I vividly remember that at the age of twelve I dreamed of having an elegant woman one day: a smiling, intelligent, wise, elegant and very happy woman with thin hands. I would find all that ten years later.

You have an excellent book in your hands meant for couples´ relationships, especially those who wish to build a successful family.

Dr. Adriana Calabria, describes her experiences in life which have helped her to affirm four testimonies: She believes in Jesus Christ, has been married for more than 30 years, has three children and two grandchildren, plus a daughter-in-law and a son-in-law. All of them serve Jesus Christ, assist and strengthen people.

I can assure the readers of this interesting, successful and strengthening book that they will find principles of life that will help them to improve and be happy every day.

You will be able to know, through the pages of this book, a fascinating and splendid woman who is always cheerful, sensitive, very positive, and self-confident. She is also a good companion, confidant, friendly,
faithful and a loyal woman. You will discover a fighter who never gives up and always trusts God.

I introduce to you my beloved wife, Dr. Adriana Calabria, whom I love with all my heart.

Apostle Osvaldo Díaz
Founder Apostle
Celebration Osvaldo Díaz Ministries (CODM)
North Carolina, USA.

Secrets to be successful

The family spiritual inheritance came to my family more than 100 years ago through my maternal grandparents. I grew up in a home that understood "family is a treasure" of the Eternal God. We are eight children who have successfully persevered in our marriages. All of us have been happily married to the same spouse for more than 40 years.

We have found the secrets of marriage and family success in the Bible. We have found secrets to be suitable spouses and secrets to respect and empower our spouses.

Men discover the value of the woman that God has given them and they give her the place she deserves. We have seen wonders in the financial administration at home and in the Ministry, as well as in the education of our children and grandchildren.

When I read Dr. Adriana Calabria's book, I was filled with joy. Nothing is better than reading the content of this book, as we live in a society where marriage and family have collapsed. The pages of this book are like balsam and fresh water in the desert. Those who read it will receive wonderful victory pieces of advice which will be helpful to them to build their marriages and families today.

I definitely recommend reading and studying it. Amen!

Apostle and Prophet Rony Chaves
Wordwide Missionary Advance
Costa Rica

Man's greatest frustration: Not understanding his wife

This book provides divine advice so that God's will is fulfilled on earth regarding male and female relationships as the basis God has chosen to show his image, character and nature. Many things are being restored and family is the most important one. If we want it to function as God has designed it, priesthood in men and wisdom in women must be restored.

I pray that each reader´s heart may be healed when taking this treasure in his hands and also, that he can come closer to God and his Word to become a better man or a better woman. Both of them must understand that it does not matter what they have got individually. It is the joint effort that makes the difference.

Pastor Magie de Cano

Author of the Devotional
Las Cartas de Magie (Letters of Magie)
Guatemala

If your marriage is going through a crisis, it means that you have to pay attention to it. Many marriages' mistake is not to look for ways to solve the situation. The correct way is to seek God, to surrender all our burdens to him so that God's will be fulfilled in our lives and marriages. If you are reading this Christian book, you must be sure it is not by chance. I do not believe in coincidences. Reading books like this one and, especially, God's Word, will eradicate all kind of crisis in marriages. Every crisis in your life will eventually end, bringing peace, joy and freedom in your family, even when you are undergoing difficult trials.

God will convince you that there is no solution and no hope without him. You need to depend on him. God will take care of you, your children and your marriage if you believe in him and are willing to let him be your priority. You must seek him.

God will help you overcome the problems you are facing in your marriage. You will be able to forgive those offenses that caused you to hurt each other and be on the brink of divorce. It is never late to rescue your marriage. The Lord wants to do it. Are you willing to do your best? Take time to read and study God's Word each day. He will give you the wisdom, self-control and a special attitude to apologize to someone you might have offended and to forgive your offender.

Every married couple should read this book as it will be very useful for their marriage relationship.

Evangelist Cielo Ortuño

Orlando, Florida

¿How do you think the future of your marriage will be?

You know, Adriana? You and I have something in common: We regard God as the center of our marriages. We understand that we have to design a future of solidarity, love and big projects in common.

My dear reader, you will discover through the pages of this book that we are not alone. You will learn the keys to understand more and you will be able to recreate your life by choosing the way to design your future. You will be able to understand that the blank page you have in front of you can be completed with blessing.

How wonderful God´s view about women is! You feel free when you think of God´s view about women. It is not only what you have been told, it is not only what you think; it is also what the Creator thinks of you; it is the reason why you have been created. We have been God's desire to bless and complete others.

You will think and feel differently once you have learned the meaning of the word "helper". It is much deeper and more powerful than what we understand today. It is wonderful! Adriana leads us to the point of understanding God's design. As a woman, you will find a new value in your purpose. As a husband and administrator in marriage, you will be able to enter a new level of commitment according to God's will.

I celebrate with resounding applause when I see a woman of the stature of Dr. Adriana Calabria. She is committed to developing contexts so that we can grow, have a broader perspective, develop our being, enhance our relationships and feel complete.

This book is meant to strengthen the view of man and broaden the knowledge of woman about man´s soul; likewise, to increase the ability to understand each other effectively and profitably.

I am sure that chapter after chapter the music of your life will sound better and you will be able to start writing your best story.

Laura Teme
Founder and President of METODOCC
Author of **Conviértete en un éxito fracasando (Become a success by failing)**
Miami, Florida

DEDICATION

Thank you, Lord, for choosing me to serve you in this time. You have inspired and given me the wisdom and conviction to believe that I can be writer.

This book is dedicated to my husband, Apostle Osvaldo Díaz, because he has inspired me to help so many men who feel frustrated and need to get to know women.

You are so strong, resolute and self-confident that I always say:**I love and admire you.**

Italics and bold in the text are used by the author to emphasize.

Edited by: Ofelia Pérez

OfeliaPerez.com

Man's greatest frustration: Not understanding his wife

A book for men that every woman must read

ISBN: 979-8-218-02484-0

Printed in the United States of America

© 2021 by Adriana Calabria

Adriana Calabria Publishing

Translation into English: Gladys Raquel Hernández

GRATITUDE

I am deeply grateful to the Heavenly Father, Jesus Christ and the Holy Spirit of God who have revealed to me what I have written in this book. How I love your Word, Lord!

Thank you, my beloved husband for having helped me to be calm and at ease to write this book.

Thank you, my beloved children, daughter-in-law, son-in-law and grandchildren because you are my reason to continue creating every day.

I am deeply grateful to each of my intercessors who have strengthened me in difficult times. They are very special and important to me.

I am also grateful to all the men and women of the CODM USA ministry because I have learned from each one of them what it means to have a spiritual family. I appreciate you all deeply!

Finally, I am grateful to Dr. Xavier Cornejo and my publisher, Ms. Ofelia Pérez, because, although I have never met them personally, they were my counselors in the art of writing and editing books. I bless you.

CONTENT

CONTENT

PROLOGUE

Man's greatest frustration... makes us think of the first months, perhaps years of marriage, when the husband thought that he understood women until he and his wife lived together. Even though women have a lot in common, we are not all the same. Honoring the commitment of true marriage love helps man to understand his wife. The conviction of the commitment before God inspires man to understand and even to enjoy the woman that God has given him as his lifesaver.

This is not an ordinary marriage advice book. It comprises experiences of everyday life. Dr. Adriana Calabria shares her experience as couples' counselor and her personal story. As she says, when we merge with our husband in agreement and commitment, we get to know and love each other deeply and share everything at all times.

We have created a three-string bond which is incorruptible and impossible to break. We have become one person emotionally, mentally, physically, and even more importantly, spiritually. When a man loves his
wife, he gets to know her and understands her; and she manages to find in her husband the protector who makes her feel secure during the difficult times of her life.

Those marriages that live a ministerial life face the challenge to be witnesses of the Lord's promises and faithful to God's Word.

We must apply his Word to our marriage, children, friends, and relatives wisely. We also have God's supreme calling and the important responsibility to be a
model to be followed not only by the members of our local congregation, but also by those who are close to
us.

We can only fulfill the commitment we have made with God through God himself and his Word as the center of our marriage commitment. Furthermore, only when husband and wife commit to understanding each other, can they create a happy union that is a good testimony to their children and to people all over the world. Man's greatest joy must be to understand his wife.

This book is intended to those people who plan to get married, to just married couples, to happy couples, and especially, to couples who are considering options that they will dismiss after reading this book.

Omayra Font
Author of best seller books
Pastor, "Fuente de Agua Viva" Churches
Puerto Rico and Florida

PREFACE

Writing a book by God's command is something one cannot escape from. I realized God was calling me to do this after having traveled to many countries all over the world for more than two years.

When I preached with my husband in Central America, people who had never met me before came to me and would said: "You have to write books."

On another occasion, in a church in Uruguay, I heard the voice of a woman sitting behind me who told me: "God tells me that you have to write books."

Likewise, in South Africa and in Nigeria (Africa) God always sent people to tell me the same thing: "You have to write."

While I was living in Portugal (European Union) I finally began to write this book. One day early in the morning, God gave me the title: *Man's greatest frustration: woman*. Afterwards, the title of the book was changed slightly to provide a more direct message.

I have always been interested in human relationships. I realized that there is a lot to talk about men and women, and to delve into the complexity of each.

This book is intended to fill a huge hole in men´s hearts who try to understand women in all the wonderful aspects of their personalities. It is not an easy task. However, allow each chapter to take you through the depth of her heart, and yours as well. You will be able to carry out the necessary changes to live a blessed and happy life.

I wish I could reach every frustrated and tired life and set up a precedent for you and your future generations.

I have included every topic: manliness, jealousy, anger, unfaithfulness and the different stages in life that men and women go through.

It does not matter if you are single or married, young or mature. This book will transform your life and you will be considered a lively and attractive man by those people around you. You will be a good father to your children. Your life will no longer be frustrating for you but it will be relevant and outstanding.

"So do not fear, for I am with you; do not be dismayed, for I am your God. I will strengthen you and help you; I will uphold you with my righteous right hand". (Isaiah 41:10)

God be with you.
Dr. Adriana Calabria

INTRODUCTION
Believe that change is possible

When I was a little girl, I used to ask my dad two questions when he was watching a movie and we were talking about an actor: "Did he die?" and "Did he get married?".

I think those were a man´s two key conditions from my point of view. At present, when I watch a show or a movie, I have to know about the actor's or main character's life. I am deeply interested in his personal life. I am also interested in singers' or musicians' lives.

This is my first book and its title has made some people smile. Some of them have even laughed because they consider it true: Man's greatest frustration: not understanding his wife.

I want to clarify that I will specifically write about the relationships between men and women, considering how God has created us. Understanding the reason for individual behavior of man and why he often acts in certain ways. There are many books that talk about women and very few about men. However, I am sure this one will catch your attention.

I have an excellent husband and a loving son. We regard our Italian son-in-law as a true son. My father is in my memory as someone exemplary. I also have the spiritual legacy of my Italian grandfather: I serve the Lord thanks to him. In addition to my personal knowledge, my experience of many years ministering to marriages and many women alike got me to delve into this exciting topic: Man's soul that wants to get to know and interpret woman's heart. I am also going to refer to marriage, children and different ages: teenagers, children and young people.

We have a very big project from now on.

There are very important things people have to understand in order to develop these topics: Man has been created by God, woman was formed by God from man, and each of them have a specific and different function.

They make the biggest mistakes and have serious difficulties in interpersonal relationships because they don't perform the tasks that each one has to do and do not obey the role established by God properly. Of course, the enemy takes advantage of this whole situation to destroy individual lives, marriages and complete families.

Many people resort to God because of interpersonal relationship problems and, especially, due to difficult situations they do not know how to solve.

In other words, if there is something that leads a man to seek God, it is a situation that causes him so much pain that he becomes impotent and does not know what to do.

Then he resorts to God as never before.

The title of this book is: *Man's greatest frustration: not understanding his wife*. It is not a book to criticize women or men, but to teach why man often feels frustrated with woman and doesn´t understand how to treat her.

Sometimes man does not know how to cope with crisis, how to please her, and ends up feeling desperate. This book will be helpful to those men who find that conflict and dissatisfaction are constantly present, because it will help you identify the most important needs of women and satisfy them. The deeper the knowledge someone has about something, the better the results he will obtain.

Get ready to start reading an exciting book.

It is high time to make a change!

GOD HAS CHOSEN US AS MAN AND WOMAN 1

"The more you get to know yourself, the more you will understand others, especially, women".

Someone who is chosen is someone who has the favor of God and receives all the benefits that his Word provides. Remember that He is the One who has first loved and chosen us.

You have been chosen to receive all the good blessings that God has prepared for you. Therefore, it is very important to focus on yourself and forge your inner world. We have to stop on the path of our life, stay still and see that, to continue moving forward in life, we must stop.

We have to be private investigators of our own lives because there is a big difference between who we are and what we do. We must look inside ourselves, because maybe there is something unresolved that does not bring you peace.

We criticize ourselves and others due to frustration because we pay attention to what we do and what others do. However, it is always easier to disagree with others than to change. Some people change for a period of time or due to pressure, but it is not a true transformation and causes frustration.

Therefore, if you meditate on your behavior regularly, you will tolerate the attitudes of other people and you will realize that you are someone who also needs to make a real change.

What we do is a consequence of who we are.

Ask yourself: Who are you? Some people do not know themselves, and love themselves excessively. They are either proud or consider that everything is wrong in their lives; so they get discouraged. This is why the Bible establishes: *"The heart is deceitful above all things ..."* (Jeremiah 17:9)

The more you get to know yourself, the more you will understand others, especially women: the central issue of this book.

It is very important to take care of your inner world, your spiritual life!

It all starts with a thought. What happens when bad thoughts come to our mind? What if those bad thoughts are pondered on too much? Thoughts are the beginning of future actions.

Every bad thought not dismissed immediately will bring bad consequences. It is very easy to think badly. It is difficult to think well. God's Word establishes in the Book of Proverbs 12:2 *that the Lord will condemn those people who devise wicked schemes* .

Therefore, the most wonderful thing about being in God's ways is we give him all our defects, faults, our situations and our problems. Thus, He gives us his justice and his love.

Furthermore, when you are a true Christian, you consider it is a blessing to be faithful to the Lord. Rejecting the worldly life and flesh, and glorifying God. Thus, the Holy Spirit of God occupies the most important place in your life. It is a moral change for a Christian person to grow spiritually in the knowledge of God´s word. It is not an intellectual capacity. It is a new life.

EVERY BAD THOUGHT NOT DISMISSED IMMEDIATELY, WILL BRING BAD CONSEQUENCES

When you get to know God more and more, you are transformed day by day. Then, from a greater knowledge of the Lord and of yourself, you will be able to change your actions and your life.

This example was taken from a message written by Watchman Nee. It is a popular story.

A few years ago, I read a fable about a centipede and a toad. The toad asked the centipede: "When you walk, which foot do you move first?" When the centipede tried to determine which foot it used to start walking it could no longer move. Then, tired because of the effort, it decided not to think about it anymore and said goodbye. But when it started walking, it tried to guess which foot it had moved first and this again immobilized it. Suddenly the sun appeared through the clouds and when the centipede saw the sun rays, it was very happy and ran towards it. It forgot completely the order in which it moved its feet.

Conclusion: The more we try to analyze ourselves, the less we can move and the more we go back. However, when we look at the light of the Lord, we advance without even realizing it.

This fable is a clear example of what happens in our Christian life. We only advance when we look at the Lord. When we pretend to look at ourselves with our own lens, we are immobilized and go nowhere. Two things happen: we appreciate ourselves excessively, or we feel too discouraged. Therefore, we must treat all people well in order not to be frustrated.

PEOPLE JUDGE US MORE ACCORDING TO OUR ATTITUDES THAN OUR INTENTIONS

The woman who is well treated is an extraordinary woman. The children who are loved will always be a blessing. However, when a man and a woman do not live happily, when they do not tolerate each other and have long-term frustrations, the stability of their relationship is at stake. This should not lead you to resignation. On the contrary, you must learn to handle everything correctly.

26

People judge us more according to our attitudes than our intentions.

The Bible establishes in the Book of James 4:17 that *"If anyone, then, knows the good they ought to do and doesn't do it, it is sin for them"*.

Many people spend their time trying to do what is fair, but then they do not put it in practice. Others know what God wants for their lives and in spite of it, they don't do it. God´s Word establishes that it is very bad to do nothing.

God´s work in your life will reach the rest of the generations that come after you, transcending towards the eternal life.

It is my desire that you can make great changes in your life after reading this book. I wish that you, as a man, feel happy, loved, valued and admired.

I think change is possible. Do you?

KILLING "MANHOOD"

2

"God wants to work through men. The devil's main goal is to kill "manhood" and many women kill that essential quality of man due to their bad past experiences".

This issue is important to understand an evil matter that manifests today and that many women do not take into account. They always blame men for everything. How men suffer!

Men have a need for affirmation, to ensure their position of power. It is something innate. God made him that way.

For this reason, every day each man makes an effort to find his place in this new order, an order that many times women change. Causing them to treat their husbands like a child and control them.

Couples long to have children and afterwards they do not raise them properly because they have too much work, yet a child needs both parents. It has been statistically proven that many homes do not have a father. There is not a man in the house and God wants to work through men.

Furthermore, we notice a new phenomenon every day. When couples get divorced, men disregard their responsibilities with their children, leaving everything in charge of the woman. Women, due to the maternal instinct and her emotions, will always take care of those children. In certain situations, she has no option other than to find a balance between her work and home. But the question is: How much blame does the woman have?

If we pay attention to the biblical model, currently there is a disorder, a bad performance of the man-woman tasks established by God. There are also obligations that each one must get to know and fulfill.

IT WILL BE IMPOSSIBLE TO KILL THE "MANHOOD" OF A MAN WHO KNOWS GOD

It is always women who complain most about men. They should stop and consider whether they have become too independent, interested in other matters, thus, underestimating whom they should care for most.

In other words, if a man obeys God and lets Him guide his life, then the woman will follow the man and even obey him.

The true man

The best example must always be Jesus Christ and how He has an excellent relationship of submission and obedience with the Father. If you, my good man, have had a good relationship with your earthly father and have been obedient to him, then you will have no problem obeying God.

And you, my good woman, find out what the man's family is like and that will show you what he is like. According to his behavior with his parents at home, so will the man be as husband and father of the family.

The man who is connected with God as Father is a true man because he will show that God reigns in his life and home. He will have his family relationships in order, love, patience and trust. A true man is generous. He always provides for his wife and children because he has learned that from his Heavenly
Father. God is loving and generous. You are His adopted son. You have all rights as a son. How superb God is!

> "*If you then, though you are evil, know how to give good gifts to your children, how much more will your Father in heaven give the Holy Spirit to those who ask him!*" (Luke 11:13)

I have ministered to countless women who have absence of the necessary conditions. They are married to selfish men who only think about themselves because they have not had a father as a model to learn in life. That's the reason why men need to get to know and love the Lord because He is the only perfect model of true love. It is a sacrificial love that gives everything and does not expect anything in return.

It will be impossible to kill the manhood of a man who knows God, connects with him and lets God transform him until he can imitate the perfect model and give his family the paternity of the Lord on earth.

The book of Romans, chapter 13, verse 8 (NLT establishes the following:

> *"Owe nothing to anyone, except*
> *for your obligation to love one another".*

Love and complement

Love is about giving and receiving. I sow love and I reap love. I give and then I receive. However, there is a deeper level of love which is the love that one gives without expecting anything in return. One does it for love, for the pleasure of love. It is the desire to give. It is the kind of love that does not expect anything from another person.

My husband is a man who feels passion for everything he does. But he is someone who truly loves me and our children. He constantly shows it through words and attitudes.

Many women kill a man's manhood due to their bad past experiences, because their dad or another men have harmed them. Thus, she does not allow him to perform his role as protector. It is natural for a man to wish to protect his wife. He even wants to be her hero.

I am a person who is easily startled and I am always grateful to God because my husband is very brave. He never gets scared about anything. He is my hero.

Every woman needs security and protection. She wants to ensure that she is the only one and the center of her husband's world. She needs to be affirmed in this area.

It is important to take into account that many women could not live their childhood as such. Life has made them grow quickly.

EVERY WOMAN NEEDS SECURITY AND PROTECTION

They have spent their lives deprived of their childhood. They did not have the possibility to be innocent. They could neither trust anybody nor learn what sincere love is. You, as a man, have to know that she is in need of your help to overcome her traumas.

Even though a woman has been deprived of her childhood, her past cannot be changed. However, she can look to the future and cling to a new life with Jesus Christ. I have always taught my daughters to enjoy each stage of their lives. Parents are placed in this world to take care of their children and ensure that they grow healthily.

Men and women are frustrated due to many reasons. One of them is that they fight a constant battle. That is not the purpose for which God has created them. God has created man and woman to complement and love each other and to live in his presence. Love is the basis of all human relationships.

Every man responds to a woman's flattery and kindness. This is not a threat for him. On the contrary, it encourages him to go out every day to do his work joyfully.

When a woman decides to compete with a man, she goes out of God's order created for her. In addition to receiving God's love, the woman must also be willing to receive the love of a man. She must be kind and gentle. She must move him through a smile rather than through an aggressive response. This does not mean that she will lose her position in life; quite the contrary. It is high time to end prejudice.

EVERY MAN RESPONDS TO A WOMAN'S FLATTERY AND KINDNESS

Many good men suffer for the love of a woman and have been abused by women who associate pain with memories that have been tormenting them since a very long time ago.

Jesus Christ wants to free women. He wants to free her so that she can love God, but also her husband and life. The man who loves this woman will help and love her no matter what the circumstances may be. He will prefer her more than anything else. He will give up everything to get to know and help her. He will even give up everything he owns as he regards her of great value.

Therefore, the first thing a man must learn is the way he has been created.

Being selfish is also destructive. Immediate satisfaction is long term destruction.

Man needs reaffirmation. Woman needs assurance that she is the only one and the center of her husband's world.

THE WAY YOU HAVE BEEN CREATED

3

"You are a divine design. Therefore, God wants you to know your origin because He has created you with his hands".

When God decided to create you, He did not do so like the other species He made "according to their kind", but God said:

> *"Let us make mankind in our image, in our likeness"*. (Genesis 1:26).

You are extraordinary because you are a divine design. For that reason, God wants you to know your origin because you have been created with his hands.

Now, God is the one who best defines manhood because He was the one who has created man:

> *"So, God created mankind in his own image, in the image of God he created them; male and female he created them.* (Génesis 1:27).

Man has been created by God for his glory and man must get to know him. As his Word is always addressed to human beings, it is there where we can confirm the way God has created man. God has formed woman from man.

Remember, He has created you, but He has formed her through you. That's powerful! God is a God of order.

The title of this book refers precisely to the frustration of men who do not understand women. But how can you understand a woman without knowing yourself first? Right?

Therefore, we must always go to the source of our knowledge: God´s Word.

> "*Then the Lord God formed a man from the dust of the ground and breathed into his nostrils the breath of life, and the man became a living being*". (Genesis 2:7).

God the Lord was who breathed the breath of life on you. Furthermore, He gave you the ability to choose. You have own free will unlike the rest of the created beings. Although all beings created by God have own life, when He breathed the breath of life into man, He printed immortality in his soul and spirit.

> "*The Spirit of God has made me; the breath of the Almighty gives me life*". (Job 33:4).

How wonderful it is to be aware that God´s potentiality has been blown into man's life! It is extraordinary to think that the[1] Zoe life of God, the abundant life is in you.

1   Zoe refers to the divine, uncreated, incorruptible, indestructible and eternal God´s life: the original life that God imparted to man before the fall. The tree of life represented Zoe´s life, God´s life.

That is, it is not only physical life, but eternal life, spiritual life, here and now in fullness, and future life of glory.

Therefore, you must understand and know your fate taking into account that God acts in your favor. Your fate is to know him more and more. It is to adore and seek him every day of your life because He is your Creator.

> "For since the creation of the world God's invisible qualities—his eternal power and divine nature—have been clearly seen, being understood from what has been made, so that people are without excuse".
> (Romans 1:20).

When you observe God's creation, you have to recognize that it is a clear and complete evidence that He exists. Every quality we find in human beings has to do with the image and likeness of God in them, even taking into account their essential value as the highest point of God's creation. For that reason, it is very important to recognize our Creator as such. It is our obligation to always improve in all areas of our lives.

Man has been taken from earth and created by God. When I learned about it, I was very surprised. Men always need to explore the outside, to be outside the house, as he has been created from earth by God. For that reason, every man has a wild and adventurous side.

Women do not understand that. She does not understand that going fishing, playing football, soccer or competitive games are part of his essence.

When you have sons, they want to run around the house since they are young children. They even love throwing cushions to one another and provoke their father to start a hand-to-hand fight because that is their wild side. It is normal.

The hero of your home: protection and service

I just want to give an opinion about how images or paintings about Jesus Christ have always been shown to us; As someone weak, very thin, and without any strength. The movie I most liked about Jesus' life was The Gospel of *John* because the actor did not have

EVERY QUALITY WE FIND IN HUMAN BEINGS HAS TO DO WITH THE IMAGE AND LIKENESS OF GOD IN THEM.

any of those traits. Quite the opposite. The movie showed a strong, brave Jesus, a warrior as it is established in the Book of Isaiah 42:13: *"The Lord will march out like a champion, like a warrior..."* and the whole chapter refers to the Messiah.

What struck me the most the first time my husband hugged me was they way I felt. That day I decided that he was the man of my life. I cannot forget that moment. I felt so much protection. His arms completely surrounded my shoulders and gave me a feeling of strength, of confidence.

And that is the way he is.

Therefore, you have to show that you are a strong, brave and hard-working man. Not all heroes in movies are really heroes. It is the culture of the world that makes you believe it. A true hero is the one who can go on living with the same woman and make her happy during all her lifetime.

Since the woman has been taken and formed from man, she needs to have a home. She has the ability to nest. Consider that she can carry a baby in her womb for nine months. Therefore, you must try to buy a house for your wife and children. A woman feels really satisfied when she has her own house which she will later turn into a home.

A TRUE HERO IS THE ONE WHO CAN GO ON LIVING WITH THE SAME WOMAN AND MAKE HER HAPPY DURING ALL HER LIFETIME

I remember when my husband and I had to rent a house temporarily on some occasions during our years of marriage because we used to travel throughout different countries where we set up churches. However, you do not feel as comfortable as when you are in your own home.

You invest in your home; you take care of it because it is yours. You settle down in your home.

You must do that to show your wife your true role as a man. Buy a house for her. Both of you must choose it together. Decorate it together and thank God for having given you your own home. This also brings stability and comfort to the life of the family.

Have a heart of service. Take the necessary time to carry out the pertinent repair work in the house so it looks good. Do it with affection, not grumbling.

I have also noticed that many families have lunch and dinner unaccompanied. Affective bonds are established if everybody sits down at the table to have lunch or dinner together.

DETERMINATION IS POWER. THERE IS A HIGHER POSITION WAITING FOR YOU

It also reinforces the self-esteem of each family member, especially if you sit down at the head of the table.

No one starts eating at my home until we are all sitting down at the table. We pray and thank God for the food. Then we talk and laugh at certain anecdotes or share our daily life.

You must *always choose a day to have a family meeting in order to share the Scriptures* . You will become a teacher to your children and wife by encouraging, teaching and studying God's Word. Thus, the gifts you have received by the Lord for your life's purpose will flow from inside you. God's Word establishes the following:

> "*Unless the Lord builds the house, the builders labor in vain. Unless the Lord watches over the city, the guards stand watch in vain*" (Psalm 127:1).

God´s Presence must always be in your home and you must be grateful to the One from whom all things come.

Seek the Lord every day of your life. Ask Him to examine your heart and trust Him. Do not trust all things you have already achieved.

> "*A person can do nothing better than to eat and drink and find satisfaction in their own toil. This too, I see, is from the hand of God* " (Ecclesiastes 2:24).

You must even enjoy your work because it has been given by the Lord. Work is a blessing. *You must be resolute in all your attitudes.*

Read this example. Agustín wanted to get to the position of financing administrator in the sales department. He was very young and was denied the position even though he was one of the best car salesmen and spoke Spanish and English. He taught older men than him to sell. He had a determined personality because he always managed to sell cars. No customer left the dealership without buying a car.

However, he set himself the task of reaching a unique vacant position when he was twenty eight years old. He attended all the courses dictated by the country. He travelled with his wife and young child and went to the hotels in the city where he had to take exams, and his wife helped him study.

He slept only a few hours and spent a long time in class. However, he passed his exams with high grades and was appointed finance manager. Furthermore, he was granted a notary license and a degree to act as financing manager in any state of the United States of America.

Determination is power. There is a higher position waiting for you.

Remember that if you want to find a wife and get married, you must first have a job. God first gave Adam the job of caring for and plowing the land and naming everything that moved and existed on the earth. Then God gave Eve to Adam as his wife.

Find joy in your work and in your daily awakening.

The Lord
commands you:
"Be strong and
courageous".
You can achieve
everything you set
out to achieve
guided by the
hand of God.

THE WAY WOMAN HAS BEEN FORMED

4

*"Woman is a divine invention. A
helper suitable for man to reach his
maximum potential. She is his
lifesaver".*

Woman is God's gift, a divine invention for man.
Obviously, she must always follow God's model
based on his Word.

God has created man and woman in a special way to
work together. God made the woman because
He himself saw that it was not good for the man to be
alone.

> *The Lord God said, "It is not good for the man
> to be alone. I will make a helper suitable for
> him." Now the Lord God had formed out of the
> ground all the wild animals and all the birds in
> the sky. He brought them to the man to see
> what he would name them; and whatever the
> man called each living creature, that was its
> name. So the man gave names to all the
> livestock, the birds in the sky and all the wild
> animals. But for Adam no suitable helper was
> found. So the Lord God caused the man to fall
> into a deep sleep; and while he was sleeping, he*

took one of the man's ribs and then closed up the place with flesh. Then the Lord God made a woman from the rib he had taken out of the man, and he brought her to the man. The man said, "This is now bone of my bones and flesh of my flesh; she shall be called 'woman,' for she was taken out of man." This is why a man leaves his father and mother and is united to his wife, and they become one flesh". (Genesis 2:18-24).

A man who lived as a hermit on an island in Australia for 23 years, concluded that human contact is a highly valued asset to possess. Even though he is 76 years old at present, he hopes to meet a lady who decides to live with him on the island because he recognizes that it is very sad to live alone.

I like saying that when God finished his whole creation, He saw woman and rested.

She is the suitable, adequate and perfect helper provided by God for man to achieve his maximum purpose and enhance his capabilities. She strengthens him in his weakness and helps him take the best decisions.

The meaning of the word "helper" is so important that Robert Alter, a Bible scholar and brilliant translator of The Hebrew Bible, says this is "a difficult word to translate."[2]

It means something much more powerful than just a

2   The Hebrew Bible: A Translation with Commentary 2018. W.W. Norton

THE WAY WOMAN HAS BEEN FORMED

"helper". It means "lifesaver." The more man gets to know her, the easier his life will be. The problem is that men make the mistake of thinking that they are owners; and they are just stewards of their wives' lives. They do not own anything. Everything belongs to God. Everything comes from God. For that reason, man must always thank God for having given him a wife, children, a house and goods.

I remember a young married couple. The man used to speak rudely to his wife using foul language. He underrated her, insulted her and even treated her as a prostitute. She was very intelligent, gifted, pretty and did not deserve to be treated like that. I got to know her

very well and realized how valued this young woman was. However, he treated her rudely because she made more money than he did. So, he was very envious and jealous of her.
He did not even try to make more money than she did. He just kept on hurting her all the time. Their marriage ended up abruptly. After that, he cried regretful because he had not valued the wife he had had.

IF YOU PRAY FOR A MAN, GOD WILL WORK IN THE AREAS YOU CANNOT MODIFY IN HIM

Each man will be accountable to God for everything God has given him. Very few people refer to this, because, in other words, if you use and value what has been given to you, you will make a profit from everything you undertake. But if you do not use and value what you have received from God, *"even what you have will be taken from you"*, such as the Bible establishes in the Book of Matthew 25:29.

A man must never work independently of God. It is his biggest mistake and his inevitable failure.

To the man: pray for your wife outloud, minister to her with God´s Word. Everyday make her fall in love with you by telling her kind words. This way, she will respect and submit to you. I have learned and have taught to couples that prayer connects both spouses. It is powerful because prayer in private elevates us in public and builds a better character in both of us.

MAN MUST KNOW THE PURPOSE HE HAS BEEN CREATED FOR. OTHERWISE, HIS LIFE IS MERE EXISTENCE

The woman is man's helper, praying for him all the time. I have noticed that most of the time women do not pray for their husbands. Women pray for their children, for their parents and for many other issues, but never for their husbands. If you pray for him, God will work in the areas you cannot modify. God does it wonderfully and faster than you think. That is marvelous!

When God mentions the woman in his Word, He commands her to "respect her husband and subject to him." Only when subjection endangers her relationship with God and leads her to sin, she is not obliged to obey her husband and has to obey God first. Otherwise, she must be faithful to this precept.

50

The woman who loves God will always obey His commandments. During my ministerial experience, I have seen many women who make decisions because men take a comfortable position: they do not obey God and do not perform the role established by Him.

Women are often disqualified by men and even often by their own husbands. Mockery, rejection and contempt are poured daily on women´s sensitive heart. When a woman gets tired and makes the decision to leave her husband definitely, she does not go back.

It is not that she does not cry out to God for her calamity. She has already cried out fot a long time; she has endured too much humilliation.

Your character is forged through family relationships: dad, mom, siblings, relatives and place of birth. One of man´s biggest needs is to know his identity: "Who am I?" It is through the deep knowledge of God, you allow to put on the "new self", created - as the Bible establishes- : *"to be like God in true righteousness and holiness"*. (Ephesians 4:24).

There are times you feel dead. Even though you still breathe, your energy and enthusiasm have vanished due to the pressures of life. However, this also happens
because you do not know yourself. Man must know the purpose he has been created for. Otherwise, his life is mere existence. You are not the result of an accident.

Osvaldo is the fourth child in his family. When he was in his mother's womb, she, in ignorance and because she already had three children and many economic needs, worked carrying buckets and heavy bags in the field where she lived so that her pregnancy would end. She would even hang from the wooden braces of the roof of the house, but nothing happened. It seems that this child was destined by God to be born because her pregnancy continued.

Osvaldo always remembers this story because his mother told him about it. She even told him that he had been her most beautiful child. When he was an adult and God dealt with his life, one day a prophet told him this Word from God:

> "Before I formed you in the womb I knew you, before you were born, I set you apart; I appointed you as a prophet to the nations." (Jeremiah 1:5).

That's when he truly understood the story his mother would always tell him.

How many places Osvaldo went through in his tender youth! He even wanted to be a mercenary. Since it was not God's plan for his life, he could not stay in the institution as he failed due to eye-related problems.

Today he is the most intelligent and knowledgeable person about Scriptures I have ever known. He is a spiritual leader and founder of international religious ministries and a Christian University.

Many people have been helped by this faithful servant of God. He lives in the country where he has always dreamed of living and has a beautiful and blessed family.

When you discover your life's purpose and fate, God forges your true character because He will use you for His glory afterwards. This is why He always takes care of you and will protect you even from death. When you let God work in your life, you will also have right relationships with everyone.

The most wonderful thing is that God will give you the right woman because his will is *"good, pleasing and perfect"*. (Romans 12:2). God does not take into account your social background *"for God does not show favoritism"*. (Romans 2:11). God has called us to live in peace and according to his Word. The Bible establishes the following:

> *"Your word is a lamp for my feet, a light on my path"*. (Psalms 119:105).

This has a very profound meaning, because in ancient times, people tied a lamp to their feet to light up the path wherein they moved. You must consider that life is quite difficult without a guide. God's Word is that guide.

God's Word is like purifying fire and like a hammer that breaks man's hardness. You must treasure his Word in your heart. His Word turns a simple person into a wise person. It strengthens your life and brings defenses in your spirit.

*Trust God more
than ever before.
Seek him daily
and let him work
in your life.*

ANXIETY, ANGUISH, ANGER, RAGE

5

"Emotions may betray you. Therefore, you must act according to your convictions. Every argument must be useful for the couple to reach an agreement and improve daily coexistence".

All of us always get angry about something or with someone. First, we must consider that anger is one of our natural emotions to react before something unfair or to try to change a situation.

When anger causes you to react or explode, that will really be a problem. You must get to know yourself and be aware of the situations or people that make you angry more easily.

Every argument must be useful for the couple to reach an agreement and improve daily coexistence. Husband or wife is the person with whom one gets angry more easily because he or she is the person with whom you spend most of your time. God´s Word establishes the following: *"In your anger do not sin: Do not let the sun go down while you are still angry"* (Ephesians 4:26. That could be translated as "don't be angry the whole day ".

Moreover, when one is in Christ, rage, anger and arguments grow because Satan, the enemy, is a specialist in fostering arguments and problems.

Marriage is a fertile ground for this because both spouses themselves as they are. There is no way to hide even if they sleep in the same bed and look to the opposite side.

SHE LIKES KNOWING THAT SHE IS ALWAYS ON YOUR MIND

It is much better to be calm, in peace, especially women, because it is difficult to get a change in oneself, and we always believe that the other is to blame.

I want to mention my husband as an example, because when we get angry about any circumstance, he is a person who immediately forges. If he has made a mistake, he apologizes at once. In other words, he does not give place to anger.

That attitude has always been very positive during all our years of marriage, because it avoided many problems in our family. I have learned a lot from him in this respect. Even when he scolded our children and corrected them, he hugged them and told them that he was correcting them because he loved them. That managed to keep our hearts healthy.

I think that God is in favor of these attitudes. He wants us to promptly take the initiative to solve problems.

Men can distinguish well when evil forces are attacking their wives. You must spend more time with her. She likes knowing that she is always on your mind, that you choose a beautiful dress and imagine her in it; that you like to hug her. When a man falls in love with a woman, he spends a long time with her and fills her personal spaces. To avoid anguish and arguments, do not keep secrets from her.

Entrust your credit card and bank account numbers to her. Entrust her with the finances for her to manage. Many women are better in this area than men. Let her see your cell phone. Surely, only if you have something to hide, you will not do it.

Two stories

Marilina was deeply in love with Ernesto. She would kiss and hug him. Every day they used to walk many kilometers along the beach.

They were inseparable. They had started dating a few months before. He had asked her to marry in front of witnesses and her parents. He made a big sacrifice to buy her an expensive ring and gave it to her (kneeling down as it is customary) with a precious bouquet of flowers. It was all a wonderful dream.

MAN'S GREATEST FRUSTRATION

One day when she was at his house, she asked him for his cell phone to take a picture of a pet. Then she saw a recent message from a woman who was chatting with him and who had made indecent proposals to Ernesto.

Of course, this situation provoked a big scandal. She spoke with his parents, with the pastors of the church where they both assisted and none of them justified what he had done. She was really shocked and her heart was shattered. He told her that he was no longer dating that woman. He asked her to forgive him. In short, he did his best to solve the problem. He even deleted all his social media accounts.

YOU MUST NEVER LET THE ENEMY USE YOUR EMOTIONS AGAINST YOU.

However, her pride was so damaged that she was never the same with him. Even though she forgave him, their relationship was thrown overboard and nothing, absolutely nothing was the same. Their romance ended. From then on, she was disrespectful towards him and he showed aggression, trying to dominate and control her.

Ana trusted Miguel in such a way that she never asked him about his earnings and the way he made a lot of money. Of course, if she did so, he would get very angry. In order to avoid arguments, she carried on with the good life they had.

He always looked at other women since the beginning of their relationship. Even though she was good looking and very intelligent, that problem continued.

He was unfaithful as soon as he had a chance, despite the repeated warnings on the part of spiritual leaders.

They were given so much advice to improve their marriage life as well as their financial life, in spite of it, they did not obey.

They suffered very much even though God had provided them gifts and talents. I am sad when I think about everything they had close at hand. Had they obeyed, today they would be very prosperous.

When people decide to do things incorrectly in any area of their lives, when they do not obey God and disregard the advice, it is impossible to turn back.

According to God's Word, Satan takes advantage of us when we are ignorant of his schemes.[3] Satan works permanently to destroy what God wants to build in your life. Therefore, you must never allow the enemy to use your emotions against you.

Alone or in bad company?

Loneliness brings a feeling of emptiness that at times becomes unbearable, generates anguish and a certain absence. Maybe you have been with that woman for a long time, maybe you have been with her for many years, but today you feel that something is wrong. Maybe it is because of the arguments or the awkward silence.

---

3 See 2° Corinthians 2:11.

However, you are still with her because, despite everything. "It is always better the evil you know than the evil you don´t", isn´t it? You know that you will feel love again because you have been with her in good and bad times and you imagine the rest of your life by her side.

The nature of man is to cling to people who may not be suitable for him because he is constantly looking for the love he does not have. If you are single, you are the result of your past experiences and of the people who have been part of your life, those who have left and those who are still there. Some of them have made you stronger and others more vulnerable.

It is said that distance makes you forget. Although you insist on forgetting those people you have loved, it is very difficult for you to get them out of your mind. Learn to hold on to what is good and reject every kind of evil. It is biblical.

Take the initiative to receive the blessings that God has prepared for you. Keep firm.

DIVORCE IS NOT ONLY SEPARATION

6

"Love affairs are just adventures, and they have an expiration date. Man always returns to a safe harbor: his wife."

Divorce is not just a mere separation. It means to uproot something that was unified. The Bible establishes the following: *"Therefore what God has joined together, let no one separate ."* (Matthew 19:6).

God has established marriage as something permanent and as the foundation of society. The devil always reveals the faults and defects of the spouse. He puts negative thoughts on the other spouse, induces to jealousy, sows suspicion and what is even worse, he makes the man or woman think that he or she would be better with someone else.

Many men divorce because they feel disappointed with the woman they married. They do not understand that they have to cultivate their wife. They cannot lose their romanticism, but must look for a new way to love. In other words, they must reinvent themselves every day. They must understand that she is their priority, the one with whom they have to spend more time with. For this reason, courtship is so important because it is the period previous to marriage, and that is where the necessary care must be taken to choose the right partner.

I remember a young man who asked us for advice to marry a girl. We asked him why he wanted to marry her if he was not sure about the step he was going to take. He said he wanted to marry her "so as not to be alone". Unfortunately, some Christians would rather marry someone who is not a believer than being alone. Of course, they have to marry someone they like and with whom they get along well. But they don't have to do it to avoid loneliness. Otherwise, they will suffer during their lives.

I can say according to my experience in marriage, that when the right person comes to your life, it is wonderful because you feel secure that he or she is the correct and suitable person for you. 2° Corinthians 6:14 establishes the following:

> *"Do not be yoked together with unbelievers. For what do righteousness and wickedness have in common? Or what fellowship can light have with darkness?"*

This is a serious warning for a marriage between a believer and an unbeliever.

The example of a yoke has to do with a piece of wood that was placed on two animals so they worked together in the fields. Two oxen had to be placed. Their size and strength had to be identical because if they were different, they would both suffer.

Therefore, if a believer marries an unbeliever, they are likely to have a lot of problems. If the believer does not help the unbeliever to truly get to know God, their marriage will be a disappointment for the rest of their lifetime.

This is why the apostle Paul, throughout the text of 1° Corinthians 7, provides so many recommendations to married people, to those who are going to get married, whether they are single or widowed.

A Christian can marry.... *"Anyone she wishes, but he must belong to the Lord."* (1° Corinthians 7:39). If you love God and his Word, how would you feel if you lived with someone who did not share your belief, right?

Marriage is a combination of very good days and also a few bad ones. The imperfect becomes singular when God intervenes. There are moments of joy, pain and tantrums. But, as soon as the storm is over, you sit down and smile.

It is not difficult for a woman to please her husband once God sets her free and heals her. Marriage has been designed for this.

Naturally a woman wants to please her husband and respect him because he is her representative before God. He is her protector, the home's priest. Man must value that and must worry about forming her. You must know that nothing is enough for her. She will always ask you for something else. It is her nature.

Marriage is about having someone in the various stages of life, someone who is just a human being and who, in many situations, makes us look up and say: "God, you are the only one who can do everything." Woman and man are imperfect, but guided by a perfect God. Glory to God!

Both spouses may have had an encounter with Jesus Christ and received salvation individually. However, they may not have received a new birth in their marriage.

WOMAN AND MAN ARE IMPERFECT, BUT GUIDED BY A PERFECT GOD

They show evidence that they are believers individually, but not in their marriage.

Many marriages need to be born again. They need life; to remove all the emotional and spiritual trash that has been accumulated through the years. They must court each other again, caress each other's soul with romantic words, because marriage must be a spiritual union. Where each one has to fulfill the work that God has assigned to them.

Man must understand that he cannot delegate his role to his wife because the most important institution established by the Lord will get worse and worse through the years. Man, as head of marriage, will always go forward. Woman, like his crown, embellishes everything he does with her beauty and dignifies him before society.

The Book of Ephesians 5:28 establishes that *"husbands ought to love their wives as their own bodies. He who loves his wife loves himself"*. I think about many men who take care of their physique and do everything to look good. They must also invest in their wives. Find a way to help her lose weight and also take care of her body. That will do you good.

Marriage is very important to God. He always takes care of each one of us individually and makes us better each day for one another and even for society.

There is a glorious spiritual revelation in the Book of Ephesians 5:25 about the relationship between husband and wife and compares it to Christ and his Church.

> *"Husbands, love your wives, just as Christ loved the church and gave himself up for her"* (Ephesians 5:25).

The biblical formula establishes every marriage´s success. Those who have a good marriage can understand it because you live in peace. But what happens if the spouses have been undergoing difficult trials for a long time and one of them has to make the decision to divorce? I always say that there are homes that are heaven and there are homes that are hell.

Every decision taken when marriages divorce has different consequences. If there are children involved, it will be much more complicated. I want to be very objective in this matter and affirm that, personally, I am not in favor of divorce because I have seen many marriages restored by God´s power, but perhaps you, who are reading this book, are already divorced.

When there are dangerous and life-threatening situations, one will have to make the decision to separate because the Lord has called us to live in peace and not to live in constant war. Whenever a woman asks me for advice about divorce as a solution to her troubled marriage, I ask her to speak with a leader of our ministry whom I consider an example of someone who made an excellent decision with her husband and today they have a complete new marriage.

In general, most people separate due to infidelities or addictions that cause the couple to have serious disagreements and disputes.

Two stories

This woman was betrayed by her husband only once, that is, the first night he did not come back home. She did not wait for him to do it again, but made him prepare his suitcase with his clothes and told him to find a place to live because she was not going to tolerate that kind of attitude.

Of course, she set some rules so he could see their daughters and gave her money to support them. As a main requirement, he had to attend all church services, complete the discipleship course and be baptized. He had to obey God.

She is a really beautiful woman. She is very kind and gentle. So, there was no reason for him to be unfaithful for lack of love in his home.

Early one morning she was praying and was very anguished. She was asking God for her husband's life. She was praying that he would love her more, live with her and their daughters and assist church. Then God made her understand that her requests were wrong. She had to pray asking for her husband to first seek God, to love Him and to surrender the direction of his life to Him. Then her husband would love and respect her and he would go to church with her and their daughters.
This marriage did not take long to be restored because a radical change was noticeable in him after a month. He even asked the pastor for advice and showed real acts of repentance.

Today she says that pain and sadness was transformed into joy and happiness by God. The Lord protected her heart, her family and gave them a true, deep, strong and stable love.

Neither of them have forgotten their experience, but God was faithful to them.

Another woman whom I appreciate very much put up with a man who caused her constant harm for years. He was extremely unfaithful, a drug addict and abusive. They had several children, good jobs, but he made life impossible for her. He used to break pieces of furniture and walls. The police had to intervene many times. The court also had to intervene for the feeding of children and they had many other problems. She was even granted a special visa in the country due to her situation of abuse.

She spent many years suffering due to this situation. God spoke to her husband in many different ways. He received a prophetic word where God warned him that if he did not change his attitude towards his wife, he would lose his life.

He attended church services for a short time out of fear of the word he had received. They even had a renewal of their marriage vows and a celebration. Certainly, all of us who knew them were very happy about his great change. Not even a year later he left home again after one year, abandoning his family for twelve months. When he left, she had to look for a job urgently because he did not give her any money to support her and their children. When he came back, he made her quit her jobs because he wanted her to stay at home all the time.

She was never unfaithful to him. Moreover, she is one of the people I know who wins more souls for the Kingdom. She has never missed any services since she came to church. She is very pretty, takes care of herself and has a beautiful body. She always wears the latest fashions but is very discreet. She is very spiritual.

We had many counseling conversations with her and made her see that she had to resort to counseling in institutions because her life was in danger. However, she never decided what to do. She continued suffering because of her husband's abuse.

It was an unhealthy relationship. One day everything got worse and she decided to divorce him.

He never cared about his family. His father had done the same. The story was repeated although God gave him many opportunities to change. But he refused to do so. I think he should have never got married. He was not a man to have a family because he lived as if he were a single person.

We all know that a woman does everything for her children. She even tries to save an unsuccessful marriage.

I have known many cases like this one during all these years. However, love for oneself must be firm sometimes and it is important to learn to take decisions.

On the other hand, love affairs are just adventures and they have an expiration date. Man always returns to a safe harbor: his wife. Some men who got divorced have acknowledged that they have never known another woman like their first wife.

A couple that is about to divorce comes to God and He makes everything new. Something new is something that is regenerated. It enters a new genesis. A new beginning.

Everything that has to do with life comes from God. He is the guarantee for your marriage. However, there has to be a will on both parts, it does not work if there is only one. "It takes two to tango", as the saying goes.

Something extraordinary is rising above the horizon of your life and your marriage.

As long as you are alive, God is not done with you. Look ahead. God knew the difficulties you were going to get through and still believes in you. There is still a chance to save your marriage.

IS MAN TESTED OR APROVED?

7

"Women will always test men very subtly. Remember: she needs certainty. She needs a man with clear ideas".

Women are unique. They are always testing men. They are subtle, unpredictable and extraordinary to do this because they want to be sure of the man they have chosen. They need to know if you are reliable, cheerful, confident, intelligent, and if you have money, personality and character.

When you are both very young, money is not very important. I can assure this. There are so many illusions and youthful moments when you are 20 years old that you only want to be together and walk hand in hand. You have the intention to marry after such a beautiful and idyllic time of courtship.

However, as time goes by this changes. Women will always test men very subtly. Remember: she needs certainty. She needs a man with clear ideas. There are men who behave like children. They are playful, unstable and insecure.

My husband taught men about the fact that man is the family supporter and I liked that teaching very much. Someone who supports is someone who preserves something, who cares for it and maintains it through the years.

When a man marries a woman and the wedding party ends, it is traditional for him to carry his brand-new wife in his arms. As years go by, he seems not to be as strong as he used to be.

MAN'S REAL WORK IS TO BE THE MAIN PROVIDER OF HIS HOME

However, that is the way God wants the man to act: like the one who carries the life of his beloved wife in his strong arms.

This obliges him to maintain his spiritual peace. His strength complements her weakness.

Likewise, he is a support where she can relax completely because she knows he will defend her. From whom? Many times, from their own children.

Yes, even though it may be somewhat subtle, sometimes children are specialists in separating mother from father. When they are young children, they do it because of their tantrums and when they are older, because of the different opinions they have.

Everything that God has given to man is *"very good* ." (Genesis 1:31. I like the real concept that before God gave man a wife, He had given him a job. Work is the means by which man feels satisfied. It is not a curse. Likewise, it allows you to be the husband God wants you to be:

> "*Put your outdoor work in order and get your fields ready; after that, build your house*". (Proverbs 24:27).

In other words, a man must evaluate whether he is ready to be a husband or not.

It is in his work that he puts in practice the abilities given by God to become the financial supporter of his home. Man's real work is to be the main provider of his home. God has established it that way. If a man does fulfill this role, the Bible establishes that he "*is worse than an unbeliever*". (1° Timothy 5:8).

Furthermore, every home has to be led by the man. But some men want neither to be too weak and treated like a puppet, nor too rude and hated.

WHICH MUST BE YOUR GOAL? KNOWING HER STRENGHTS AND WEAKNESSES

God says: "*Husbands, in the same way be considerate as you live with your wives, and treat them with respect*" (1° Peter 3:7), and this comes from the Greek word that means "to build a home according to understanding and agreement."

Therefore, as I said before, man's greatest frustration is not understanding his wife.

You must know her personality. For example, I am going to describe myself so you can do the same with your wife or your future wife.

My ancestors were Italian. So, my first characteristic is that I am very talkative. That has helped me a lot. If I had to define myself, I would say I am a communicator. I have put this service in practice in the church. This was even very useful to me when I worked as a senior officer in the Federal Court.

Sometimes I had to learn to keep silent in time in order to avoid many problems because I always felt like the "know-it-all" and it wasn't always like that. So, I had to repent and understand that I was not the only wise person at home, or in my work.

HUMAN BEING'S BIGGEST MOTIVATION IS TO BE LOVED

I really like something that my husband does when I make mistakes or talk too much: he really overlooks all that... he overlooks many trivial things. That has really helped us in the routine of everyday life. He is very important to me. Well, I have the perfect husband. He always surprises me, and of course, I always surprise him.

My husband is an approved man.

So which must be your goal? You have to know her strengths and weaknesses.

Women love to be protected. She likes you to look after her and worry about where she is, what she is doing and what she needs. You must be kind and thoughtful to her. You must watch your entire family environment and supply every single need. She has to rest in you, knowing that you will plan and have clear goals about where your family will be during the years to come.

A man's vision never dies when it is in his heart. He has passion which generates power in him: It is God's true power that establishes a strong authority and perfection in everything he does.

A man who has God's Word in his life is a man who fulfills whatever he has promised. He is not afraid of failure because God's Word guides his life.

WOMEN MAKE MEN SUFFER

8

"Some men suffer for many years
without uttering a single word to the woman in his
life. This is really very harmful. However, if a man
is sincere and expresses his feelings to
his wife, their love will be stronger".

I have noticed from my own experience in counseling women that many times, they make men suffer.

When a woman becomes a private investigator of a man and his world, she forgets that she also has hidden sins. Every time women have consulted me about their husband or future husband is because they no longer feel they can fully trust them. Besides, in this era of technology and mobile phones, one cannot believe that something so useful can cause so many problems and arguments in couples (whether it is pornography, illicit friendships, etc..

Likewise, it has been proven that social media has been designed to be addictive and to create a feeling of comfort in the mind. One of the five founders of Facebook manifested this to journalism. He added that social media produced vulnerability in people's minds.

I remember the story of a young woman, influencer, who had an account on Instagram with more than one million followers. She would post her pictures taken in different parts of the world or with her boyfriend in restaurants. She also wore fashionable clothes and taught a new makeup trends. People wrote letters of affection to her, raising her self-esteem and always standing her out. Human being's biggest motivation is to be loved and to ensure that people are interested in their matters.

When she was asked if she was happy about having so many followers, she said that everything was a sham. She had an existential emptiness. Her boyfriend was unfaithful to her and her biography was not according to everything she posted on social media.

What kept her as an addict of others' opinions? The fact that people would tell her: "I love you"; "you are unique", "you are my motivation", "you are very beautiful".

There is no doubt that beauty is manifested in many ways and men like a woman´s physical appearance. However, true beauty is only skin deep. God values woman's inner beauty. Man will also value her inner beauty.

A faithful man is very much appreciated and highly valued because he is a man of covenant. He does not harm the woman he loves and his generations will be faithful as well.

We always reap what we sow. Many women do not forgive men. If we do not forgive, those who have to forgive us will not do it easily. That is very sad and painful.

There are women who have got used to pain after years of relationships and negative experiences. God establishes the following:

> "*Finally, brothers and sisters, whatever is true, whatever is noble, whatever is right, whatever is pure, whatever is lovely, whatever is admirable -if anything is excellent or praiseworthy -think about such things*". (Philippians 4:8).

Your life matters to God because He has given his own life for you.

A perfect man is a mature man who confesses his sins, repents, and never again commits them. He is a man who does not fight against a sin not confessed to God. He always keeps a clean heart.

The Book of Luke 18:1 establishes that men must "*always pray and not give up*".

This is a sincere and constant communication with the Lord. This will free you from many pains and sorrow.

God's grace will flow constantly in your life if your heart is pure.

Man will be able to give others the mercy he has received from God.

Freely you have received; freely give. Some men or women never express their gratitude. I have realized that this happens because of rejection. Those who have been rejected, especially in their childhood, believe that everybody owes something to them. They state that their lives have been unfair, that they did not deserve what has happened to them. They even blame God for that situation.

EACH ONE OF US IS RESPONSIBLE FOR THE WAY WE ALLOW OTHERS TO TREAT US

There is a biblical story that clearly shows rejection. It is the parable of the ten men who had leprosy[4]. Those men had a miserable life. They were totally rejected by society. Jesus healed all of them. However, only one of them expressed gratitude and was saved. Indeed, Jesus Christ was interested in their gratitude. For that reason, he wanted to know about the other nine men who did not return.

It is very important to be grateful. Firstly, you must be grateful to God and then to those who accompany you

---

4 See Luke 17: 11-19.

day by day. Have you thanked God for everything you have?

Marimar was not a difficult woman. On the contrary, she was obedient and even too calm, quiet and passive. She had had four children with her husband and never managed to draw his attention. He did whatever he wanted with her.

He used to date other women and drank excessively. So he used to drive drunk many times and that represented a serious danger. In addition, all the money he made was spent on drinks and women. As a consequence of this, his family suffered.

A FAITHFUL MAN IS VERY MUCH APPRECIATED AND HIGHLY VALUED BECAUSE HE IS A MAN OF COVENANT

They had been helped and advised in order to improve their marriage. In spite of their comings and goings, he could never make a real change.

It is important to notice the way I began to describe Marimar: She was obedient, calm, quiet and passive.

Today they are temporarily separated as they were on many occasions.

She was making her whole family suffer due to her weak character and attitudes. She did not establish limits from the very beginning. Why am I saying this?

Of course, I am not in favor of woman´s abuse; quite the opposite. However, there are situations that are consequences of lack of limits.

Each one of us is responsible for the way we allow others to treat us. If a woman is indifferent to a man, she will make him suffer. Of course, it wasn't that way when they got married.

Man is a natural-born reactionary. Therefore, the woman must treat him wisely because he also needs to be listened to and valued. Permanent criticism as well as mockery in public is not good, especially when the woman comments on his mistakes, even though it might seem funny. Moreover, if he goes out to work and she stays at home taking care of their children, she must thank him for every check he brings home.

A woman´s exaggerated independence makes man suffer as he already lives in his own world and has many responsibilities and obligations. He needs words of gratitude and recognition. Men depend on women emotionally and psychologically. He always wants her approval, so she must consult and entrust everything to him, even what she is going to do with their children.

Some men suffer for many years without uttering a single word to the woman in his life. This is really very harmful. However, if he is sincere and expresses his feelings, their love will be stronger.

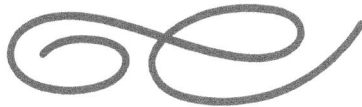

WHAT DO WOMEN NEED FROM MEN?

9

*"Male chauvinism does not make
anybody fall in love. It is outdated. It is
marvelous to wash dishes and to
collaborate in the kitchen with her. Those are
helpful attitudes. Women always fall in
love with helpful men".*

This is a very practical, real and necessary topic: getting to know what she needs from you. Even though we all need things, you have to understand that there is something that is vital for a woman: She needs to feel loved. You must spend more time in God´s presence and more time with yourself so you can show your love to her.

God´s Word must nurture your thoughts in such a way that everything you say is supported by his Word. The Bible establishes the following:

"For as he thinks in his heart, so is he." (Proverbs 23:7)

You must find a quiet place to praise God with songs, psalms and spiritual hymns. Praise Him. Praise is powerful. He has freed you and you can do it. Then it will be easier for you to love because God pours his love into our hearts.

Man is an inborn conqueror. When he has a woman, he seems not to value her any longer. That is, he feels comfortable with her and knows that she will always be there for him. Therefore, charm and passion disappear.

HOW CAN YOU LIVE WITH THE SAME WOMAN DURING SO MANY YEARS? BECAUSE OF HER CONSTANT TOUCH OF SEDUCTION AND BECAUSE SHE IS UNPREDICTABLE.

How can you live with the same woman during so many years? Because of her constant touch of seduction and because she is unpredictable. It is really marvelous to have a good sense of humor and to respect each other. All matters must always be discussed and clarified. We must not underestimate our spouse. Try it: "Listen, honey, I don't like that person. Be careful."

It is always better to establish limits with love.

Woman feels loved when she is listened to emphatically. That is to say: "Your pain hurts me", "Your joy makes me happy". Woman feels she is really loved when man takes care of her and when they walk hand in hand.

When man introduces her to people, he does it proudly: "my wife", "my girlfriend".

Woman loves service, that is, when man tells her: "Don't stand up. I'll bring it to you." Those are nice gestures.

Male chauvinism does not make anybody fall in love. It is outdated. It is marvelous to wash dishes and to collaborate in the kitchen with her. Those are helpful attitudes. Women always fall in love with helpful men.

If you put it in practice, she will not prevent you from going to play soccer, go fishing or hunting.

Woman likes a romantic and sweet man. She likes him to talk to her softly, especially knowing her nature and female hormones which change during certain days of the month.

Maybe you have become the last romantic man in history, I mean, a man who opens the car door for her, who walks along the street hand in hand or gently runs his hand through her hair. It is important that you have nice gestures and attitudes, putting aside inhibitions, after which you will have the best intimate moments with her.

A woman's sense of smell is much more intense than a man's sense of smell. It is very important that you smell very good. That attracts woman powerfully, even more than your physical beauty.

Surprise her with an invitation to go out together. If you go to a restaurant, you should make the reservation and look for a special place only for both of you, without children, and surprise her with a present. Also, tell her how much you wanted to share that time with her and how beautiful she looks. Take pictures of her with your cell phone and have a pleasant chat recalling the best moments lived with her.

It all sounds great, doesn't it? Why don't you do it often? You do not need to spend a lot of money. You can go out to have an ice cream, to walk along the city, to chat in a cafe. But you always have to do it together, just you and her. You have to continue doing the same things you used to do when you were her boyfriend.

Surely you did not show up smelling like car oil when you had to meet her, did you?

WOMEN ALWAYS FALL IN LOVE WITH HELPFUL MEN

Another important issue to keep in mind is that women may feel fulfilled or not in every stage of their lives. As regards this specific case, I am going to give an example of a woman I know, who is alone at this time. I can assure that she feels more fulfilled than ever before.

This does not mean that she has not felt fulfilled as a mother and wife. However, I believe that she has now discovered her true identity, her true inner self.

She has grown spiritually more than ever before. This means that women do not always need to have a husband or someone by their side, but they need to feel fulfilled first and then, in addition, they will be a blessing for her husband, children and even for those people around her.

For that reason, you must help her reach her maximum potential, her most desired goals.

I remember that when I had to study hard and take exams in order to advance in my judicial career, my husband helped me a lot. Not only did he take care of our three children, but when I came home from work, I did not even have to prepare dinner because he had already done everything: he had washed and ironed our clothes, had cleaned the house and had even bathed our children.

YOU MUST HELP HER REACH HER MAXIMUM POTENTIAL.

What do you think my reward to him was? My respect, gratitude and admiration; and of course, extraordinary and quality intimate time with him. That has made our marriage unshakeable.

I am deeply grateful to God because we have never failed when we counseled men and women: we have had more families restored than broken.

On the other hand, I have noticed women who have had a past life and then come to Christ but their daughters –mainly their daughters– do not. They have seen the past life of their mothers and decide to keep away from the Lord. Thus, they mirror their mothers´ behavior.

Therefore, if you decide to follow the Lord, you must truly change your life. Otherwise, your children are going to do the same you did when you still did not know the Lord. For that reason, it is said that if your children have not been better than you, you have had them and brought them up in vain.

When a Christian man or woman commits sexual sins, the fact is even more serious because people pay more attention to what a believer does than what he says.

It is high time to understand that you cannot play with God. He cannot be mocked.

Take special care of what God has given to you. Take care of your wife. If you do this, you will also take care of your legacy, your offspring and future.

WHEN WOMEN ARE JEALOUS OF MEN

10

"Jealousy is the result of the works of the flesh and of an unrenewed mind. When your imagination is healthy, it does not have negative images; there´s no jealousy".

Maybe you will be somewhat surprised by what you are about to read now: a bit of jealousy is not bad at all. It is a sign that you care about someone. However, when jealousy is obsessive, it means that you are concerned about losing that person.

The Bible establishes that God is a jealous God. Every man likes to say that his wife only belongs to him. This shows normal jealousy.

However, when a woman is jealous of a man, she is because of some insecurety, distrust and is afraid of being betrayed.

It is also true that women are jealous of men due to certain attitudes, but men do not do it intentionally. A woman is always jealous of a man's past because she wants to be exclusive in his life. She is afraid and imagines unreal things. So she thinks she is going to lose him.

A woman found a blonde hair in her husband's black scarf. So she began to follow him with her car. First she went to the office where he worked, then to the coffee shop where he had coffee every day. She saw him enter a flower shop where he bought a bouquet of flowers.

On the next stop she saw him enter the nursing home where his sick mother was. Needless to say, she had told a lot of people about this situation: her friend and
her work mates. She always needed to speak about everything. Jealousy consumed her.

The blonde hair turned out to be her husband's mother's hair. He had brushed his mother´s hair lovingly the day before. He was taking the bouquet of flowers to his mother because it was Mother's Day and he was paying tribute to her. This is a tremendous story, isn't it?

So, you must remember this. She needs to know in detail everything you do every day. That will spare you many bad moments.

On the other hand, all this is very dangerous when it gets out of control. This is why you, as a man, must give her security and protection by making her feel exclusive. Otherwise, she will control and manipulate you to such an extent that you will feel cornered.

Manipulation is evident when someone makes you think you are accountable for something you did not do. It occurs when you do not understand her attitude and wonder: "Have I done anything wrong? Have I said anything that bothered her? But her only response to you is: "You know ...".

You must calm her anxiety with love and patience. You have to tell her that you will always be there for her, that you will never abandon her.

You must be her confidant, because she can talk to you about any topic, especially because she catches your attention. You should not be distracted by anything when she is talking to you. However, you must never be responsible for something you really did not do. We must not bear the guilt of others.

Why are women so jealous? She believes that you are no longer interested in her, that perhaps you do not like her company any longer, or she does not know how to be alone without feeling bad. Therefore, she cannot share you with anyone, not even with your mom or your sister.

I know a young man who is a musician. He is a very kind, talented and an educated man. He has certain behavior with the church's sisters when his wife is there, even during rehearsals. On the other hand, his behavior is different when his wife is not there. He may not even greet any woman because of her orders. Whoops!

Needless to say, he is not a very happy young man.

For this and other reasons, you have always to tell the truth to your wife, trying not to cause her any harm.

Let her entrust her fears and secrets to you. You must never betray her.

Likewise, you must work on her self-esteem. Help her feel she is beautiful and valued through words, gestures, hugs and kisses.

YOU MUST WORK ON HER SELFESTEEM. HELP HER FEEL SHE IS BEAUTIFUL AND VALUED.

You must never let her believe she is a martyr. If she manifests jealousy of matters related to your past and projects those feelings in the present time, you will have to let her know slowly and calmly that she is not always right.

Sometimes she is jealous unexpectedly, that is, unintentionally. Therefore, she reacts angrily, frowning, with unfounded accusations.

What do you have to do in these cases? First, you must resort to prayer to find peace and shelter in the midst of a storm of feelings. Then you have to find the right moment to speak up and say the following to the other: "Listen, honey, you have really harmed me with your attitude." That is, the other person has to understand how you felt at that moment. Don't use sarcasm or exaggeration.

Jealousy is the result of the works of the flesh and of an unrenewed mind. Be reasonable. When your imagination is healthy, it does not have negative images; there's no jealousy. Talking is the best option. But you must always look for the right moment to talk and the presence of the Holy Spirit of God must be there. Both of you must always try to please Christ. When this happens, it is natural for you to forgive.

I have read this comment of the book *"Envy and Jealousy. Taming the untameable"*, written by June Hunt.

> "Praying for the person who makes me jealous or envious is the key that opens the prison door. When I have found myself trapped in the prison of jealousy, my only hope of liberation has been prayer. I had to pray for the person who made me jealous. When 'I prayed for my enemy', Christ released the prisoner and that prisoner was me!"

You will never lose what belongs to you. It will not be taken away from you for any reason whatsoever. You have just to prepare your heart to have sensitivity to do what is right and fair.

It is not fair to be jealous. It takes the person to make many mistakes. For that reason, you must pray to be free. As a result, your life will change considerably, especially when Agape love is poured on you. It is God's love.

Agape love always looks for the well-being of the other and expects everything from God and not from the other person. It is extraordinary.

IS THE PERSON WHO LOVES THE MOST ALWAYS HAPPIER?

11

"Whoever loves the most has a very high concept of other people, holds on to what is good and rejects every kind of evil. He overlooks small difficult situations and concentrates on the virtues of the other rather than in his shortcomings".

It is better to give than to receive. We have always heard this concept: but, as a man of action, you have to be willing to give.

Sometimes when I observe my journey through my married life, I can assure that my husband and I have got used to giving. I truly believe that, when you love, you have no other option than expressing it because it has to flow. Once you have given all your love to a person, then more love is generated within you.

So, if we think that the one who loves the most is happier, and we both love intensely, then we can say that we are both very happy. Likewise, if God is a priority in our lives, it is even more extraordinary, because his Word establishes that *"God's love has been poured out into our hearts...".* (Romans 5:5

How awesome this is! That makes me feel that spiritual matters are part of both our lives and a stronger union is built.

It is a spiritual union built by the heavenly model: Christ, husband, wife. Of course, it is obedience to the Lord. There is no success out of this model because God is love. Love is his essence and that comes to each of us who have accepted him as Savior.

Love is about devotion. I have heard many times my husband say that he would give his life for me if necessary. It sounds deep, doesn't it? But I believe it. I know he would do so, because I know the intensity of his love.

God's love helps us when we cannot accomplish things through our own human strength.

The one who loves the most ...

- Has a very high regard for other people.

- Holds on to what is good and rejects every kind of evil.

- Overlooks small difficult situations.

- Concentrates on the virtues of the other rather than on his shortcomings.

- Finds it very easy to forgive.

- Has a very bad memory.

- Is constantly being renewed in their mind. He/she does not conform to a model or design.

- Always makes a change for his/her own benefit and for the benefit of others.

- Is not a superficial person.

- Has great inner wealth.

- Nurtures his/her mind with God's Word.

- Has a concept of what dignity is and, therefore, he/she does not pretend to love. He/she truly loves.

- Has compassion. This is something people have really forgotten during these times of unworthiness and criticism.

When someone feels compassion, it means that selfishness will no longer take place and concern for the feelings of others will prevail. It is mercy in action. It is said that no one can give what he does not have. Therefore, if you need love, ask God for his unconditional love.

Be happy! Love!
You must
always
remember that
God's love is the
only love that
never fails
because it is
eternal. Amen.

THE LONE MAN WHO NEVER NEEDS HELP

12

"Your help, your lifesaver was closer to you than you thought. God knew that you would need someone else… "

How many times have you tried to fix that electrical problem at home and you couldn't solve it? Since there was not another man there to help you (such as your father or brother), you resorted to the Internet to consult.

Life makes us believe that people cannot make mistakes, that you are supposed to do everything perfectly. Maybe it is what you've been taught and your masculine pride keeps you from asking for help. However, it turns out help was closer than you had thought. You have forgotten that the woman God gave you is your ideal and suitable helper.

The Bible establishes in the Book of Ecclesiastes the following:

"Two are better than one, because they have a good return for their labor: If either of them falls down, one can help the other up. But pity anyone who falls and has no one to help them

*up. Also, if two lie down together, they will
keep warm. But how can one keep warm
alone? Though one may be overpowered, two
can defend themselves...*" (Ecclesiastes 4:9-12)

It means that, if you succeed, you will be able to share
your success with someone. If you fail, someone will be
able to help you. This also refers to companionship, to
sharing moments. It is about heat in times of cold
and loneliness.

It is powerful to see a man and a woman resisting the
storms of life together.

There are self-sufficient men who are very lonely.
They think: "*Ask for help? No! Men do not do that*".
God even waits for you so He can help you. This is why
the Bible establishes the following: "*A cord of three
strands is not quickly broken* ". (Ecclesiastes 4:12).

Why? Because if you have children, they will help you
and you will be stronger. You will have heirs who will
help you and stay with you until the end of your life.
You used to rely on your friends ... Friends come and go,
but if you bring up someone who has your own blood,
they will stay with you until the end. Thus, your wife
will be very happy.

This is amazing! Glory to God!

You must appreciate God´s blessings: your children and
your wife who remain with you.

Enjoy your life living wisely. The Bible establishes that
there are begotten children who do not inherit anything[5]

5 See Ecclesiastes 5:14

because of foolishness and imprudence. Their parents neither took into account nor valued the offspring given by God.

There is something real. A woman can fend for herself. God has made her that way. That is, she is able to do things and get ahead. Of course, that is not ideal. She must always have a man who complements her.
However, a man cannot get ahead alone many times. He needs someone to help him. Since he does not read instructions, the woman has the direction. She has the map that shows where he wants to go to.

IT IS POWERFUL TO SEE A MAN AND A WOMAN RESISTING THE STORMS OF LIFE TOGETHER.

Why? Because a man needs someone to teach him since his childhood, he needs someone to guide him during his lifetime. He needs God, because if he does not have God, he is incomplete. If you are a young person, don't hesitate to establish now a correct relationship with God, before the disappointments that you may face in your life harden your heart. Look for a Christian counselor because you need someone to guide and teach you in the true life: the Christian life. It is a permanent life and everything will have true meaning for you.

God wants you to be formed, He knows you won't be able to do so on your own. God wants you to let yourself be corrected. To succeed, many times you have to suffer, and then be corrected.

Life is not only about surviving. It is important to understand that God wants us to be obedient so He can give us the best.

WHY ARE YOU SO REACTIVE?

13

"If you are disobedient to God, your children will be disobedient to you".

Sometimes you may wonder ... How is it possible that I have reached this point in my life in which I attack those people I love the most verbally and physically?: My wife, my children, and even my own parents.

Deep down you are an insecure man, who has to yell or hit in order to show authority. Surely, it is a false authority because you have never earned the respect and obedience of your family. Sometimes you behave like a rebellious child. If your family does not obey your orders, you get furiously angry.

I always preach the following: "If you are disobedient to God, your children will be disobedient to you." You demand once and again, but have you thought of the fact that you don't give anything in return?

While I was watching a movie, I saw a scene in which the main character, who was a writer, discovered that his former wife, with whom he had had a son, had secretly married his best friend and partner. She never let him know about it for fear he would separate her from her son.

The writer was a very generous man. He supported his former wife and son with all kinds of luxuries and comforts. She owned a beautiful apartment, very expensive dresses, a new van and her son attended a private school. Despite being separated, he always spent time with his child and provided all that they needed. However, when he discovered the lie on part of his former wife and his best friend, he took such a strict decision that I was amazed.

Even though the movie was filmed in the Middle East, where the culture is completely different from ours, the man's attitude was to take everything:
house, van, credit cards, mobile phone, everything without any aggression whatsoever.

She then went to live with her mother and felt desperate because she believed that he would separate her from her son. However, he did not do so. She continued living with her son.

This is an example I wanted to share with you, where there is a man who gave everything for this woman and this child. Of course, he always bore in mind that she was the child's mother. He had the right to make the decision he made.

Well, those who are reading this story may agree or not with my opinion. But this writer was an upright man who decided to benefit his former wife because he loved his son.

I thought: "Maybe he did not deserve to be deceived the way he was deceived."

When you give, and only when you give, you are entitled to demand something in return, to ask for respect and reward for your work, effort and dedication to your family.

Each home has its distinctive features. But every brave, upright and honest man will have a true home and a true family guided by God's principles and moral rules.

Thus, you must seek God and faithfully assist a church where sound doctrine is preached. Your whole family will go with you. When a man does this, something powerful happens: his wife and children follow him.

This is a note taken from a digital Christian newspaper AcontecerCristiano.net, which reports the following:

> *"Couples who attend church services together may be happier than couples who do not attend. Couples who attend services, or when only man attends, are happier than couples who do not attend or when only woman attends"*, according to a study carried out by the Family Institute.

The organization's report entitled "Better Together," written by W. Brandford Wilcox and Nicholas H. Wolfinger, points out that 78% of couples who attend church services together regularly, or when only man attends, are "very happy" or "extremely happy," according to the Christian Post.

> *"On the other hand, 67% of couples who do not attend church services are happy and only 59% of couples in which only woman regularly attends church services are very happy. It is clear that when they both go together, their attendance is linked to a better quality of their relationship"* the study affirms.

Wilcox and Wolfinger affirm that the content of sermons is the reason why relationships are highly valued when only man attends church services.

> *"The results suggest that men's attendance is especially beneficial for a good relationship. This is perhaps because churches are some of the few institutions that encourage men to invest in their families,"* the study also affirmed. [6]

My husband teaches men on Fridays in our church in North Carolina. These men always receive specific and revealing teaching so that their lives and families may be transformed.

---

6 Online Consultation: https://www.acontecercristiano.net/2016/02/estudio-revela-que-parejas-son-mas-felices.html?m=1)

We have noticed a big change in each of the attendees and in their relationships with their wives and children. This confirms what has been described in the studies carried out.

We are each responsible for how we allow ourselves to be treated.

When you give, and only when you give, you are entitled to demand something in return, to ask for respect and reward for your work, effort and dedication to your family.

BUT... CAN'T YOU SPEAK TO ME APPROPRIATELY?

14

"Man is sensitive to his wife´s words of admiration. The man that shows he is shy and sullen is substantially suffering. He is fearful".

One of man´s main features is to be reserved about many of his personal affairs. He does not inform his wife about everything that happens to him. He does not do this out of lack of love, but because these attitudes are part of his way of being. He has to face his own fears and insecurities many times.

He usually expresses in a few words and accurately everything that his wife wants to know, although she always needs to know more. He always reserves something for himself. He does not express everything because he lives in a constant search for problem-solving.

I cannot help but laugh as I write this... But it must not be easy to be a man, considering how complicated women are... I include myself.

Behaviors and alternatives

Men are usually more reactive than women. Women do not understand the reason for men's reactions. This is where she has to be very wise and wait for the right moment to speak. Men do not always want to talk. Many times it is better to be silent.

When a man is bad tempered, he acts in two ways: he either reproaches or blames his wife. He also carries it over to the children.

I remember the story of a very close Christian couple. They have both studied in the Biblical institute for five years, where they met. Then they fell in love and eventually got married.

After a few years and after a long day of about 8 to 10 working hours, driving a bus throughout the city of Buenos Aires with millions of people and thousands of cars in the street, the husband finally arrived home, anguished and nervous due to the daily bustle.

At the precise moment he was entering his home his wife began to ask him to repair items in their house. He had not repaired anything in the house for a long time due to his exhaustion. Her requests turned into complaints and criticisms. Unfortunately, this couple got divorced. Their children haven´t gotten over the trauma as a consequence of what they have experienced.

Women must act in faith under those circumstances. She only has to utter a few words and must be calm. She has to know how to communicate with him in such situations, when many times it is much better to be silent and overlook anger or rage.

Sometimes silence is very appropriate. "*A gentle answer turns away wrath...*", the Bible establishes in the Book of Proverbs 15:1.

MAN IS SENSITIVE TO HIS WIFE'S WORDS OF ADMIRATION.

Men do not like direct confrontation. On those occasions he isolates himself. He may also become a fugitive and you cannot find him anywhere. This is real and many times the woman cannot interpret what is happening to him because there is no communication between them in this period.

Moreover, if you conceal... forget it! I mean if you either hide or pretend... Right? Now, you must give in and change that position. This is why the Bible establishes the following: *"Do not let the sun go down while you are still angry..."* (Ephesians 4:26).

Therefore, the woman must choose the best course of action and change the atmosphere of her home through prayer; remain silent, choose the right moment to speak. You, my good man, have to get out of your stubbornness, overlook problems and encourage communication. You should always try to take the first step. Don´t be proud and text her asking for forgiveness. When you talk to her, you must always look at her eyes, run your hand through her hair and tell her how much you love her. Make her laugh.

How to survive

Each one of us is a survivor of something or someone. I always say: "If God freed me from that situation, He will do it again". You cannot change where that problem came from, but you can change what is coming in the next stage of your life.

PASSION AND DESIRE ARE ESSENTIAL IN COUPLES.

Yes, human beings need to turn to God more than ever before. Men and women must return to their Creator's original plans for their lives through the Holy Spirit of God and through the principles of God's Word.

A man is sensitive to his wife´s words of admiration. The man that shows he is shy and sullen is substantially suffering. He is fearful.

I have seen many good men be abused by selfish women. When a man is rejected and disrespected by his wife or children, he feels a terrible pain.

Many couples continue their relationship although many situations have not really been resolved because they do not communicate. You, my dear reader, must surely feel identified with what I am saying because that's your biggest concern: not knowing which words to utter to express your feelings.

Sometimes you want to be alone, watching television or talking to a friend, answering an e-mail, or just doing nothing. As you do not express to her what you need to do, she keeps talking and talking.

The tastes of each one are not respected.

Not to mention when she only pays attention to those children who are the fruit of your love. However, now she only concentrates on them and you are invisible to her. She used to be your passionate companion and now she only takes care of those lovely little children. Well, it is the law of life. Living together does not mean that you understand each other. Everything is a matter of the heart. The Book of Matthew 12:35 establishes the following:

EVERYTHING YOU SAY MUST HAVE A CLEAR OBJECTIVE.

> *"A good man brings good things out of the good stored up in him, and an evil man brings evil things out of the evil stored up in him".*

Some men´s hearts have been damaged. Man, who has been created by God, must love with all his heart, mind, soul and body. He must love God first and then his wife. Love must be the first feeling in his heart. Then he will also love his children and will understand everything that happens around him.

In the face of despair, God!

Most divorces occur because the man does no longer loves with his heart, therefore his wife no longer respects him, and rejects him. Both of them also fall into despair due to lost passion. Passion and desire are essential in the couple. It is your daily renewed enthusiasm transmitted to her, producing in both of you the desire to be together; becoming inseparable. Test for yourself how contagious passion is.

This is why men must beg to God: "Lord, give me a new heart."

God's Word establishes in the Book of Proverbs 4:23: *"Above all else, guard your heart, for everything you do flows from it"*.

You, my good man, must understand that we are talking about a woman. You will be disappointed if you expect everything from her, when in reality you must expect everything from God. He is your source and will supply all your needs. Include God in whatever you do. You must learn to trust God and wait for his answer.
The problem is that you have no patience, and you will need to be very patient.

He will provide everything. The Bible establishes the following: *"... love covers over all wrongs "*.[7] Why? Because you have seen the worst in a person and

7 Proverbs 10:12.

120

you are still with that person. That is called love.

Hasn't God seen the worst in us and still loves us? For that reason, you must seek God at all times because He is love. Our Lord, Jesus Christ, has made the biggest sacrifice, the cross, to show us how authentic his love is.

God loves you, my good man, even when you are wrong. He heals your heart that has been full of lies. Your character has been probably built by your past experiences. We know what a person is like according to the experiences he has lived, genetics or the place where he has grown up. When one comes to Christ, He makes everything new.

Since you start to think differently, you also speak differently.
> *"For the ear tests words as the tongue tastes food".* (Job 34:3).

You cannot speak nonsense. Everything you say must have a clear objective.

There is a book written by Dr. Lucas Márquez entitled: "Talking is never an innocent act".[8]

---

8 Kindle, February 2, 2019.

In other words, what you say becomes your blessing or a curse because you receive according to what you speak. If you speak blessing, you will receive blessing because you speak well. But if you speak evil words, you will receive evil.

> *"But I tell you that everyone will have to give account on the day of judgment for every empty word they have spoken. For by your words you will be acquitted, and by your words you will be condemned."* (Matthew 12: 36-37).

Empty words are words uttered without thinking. They come to your mouth and you don't process them in your mind. How many dire consequences they bring to your life!

Our words are uttered twice: First, here on earth, then in the presence of God, when we will be judged. We will account for every word we have uttered without thinking on the day of judgment.

> *"Do not let any unwholesome talk come out of your mouths, but only what is helpful for building others up according to their needs, that it may benefit those who listen"*. (Ephesians 4:29).

"Unwholesome" refers to something in a bad condition, with a bad smell, something that has gone bad. Therefore, you must be careful about what you say. However, when God changes something in you, He begins to breathe the breath of life into your heart.

So everything begins to improve: the way you see things and the fact that you can be satisfied in everything you do.

The Church is a body and we all work together in order to help one another and carry the burden that overwhelms other brothers and sisters.

I want to specifically mention what happens in our ministry, "Celebration Osvaldo Díaz Ministries (CODM)" in North Carolina, United States. All the Ministry leaders have taken the following biblical exhortation very seriously: *"To watch over souls"* (Hebrews 13:17), thus taking care of the spiritual health of the whole congregation.

The best place will always be God's church. It is the place where we help you to build your life through the Word and testimony. The power of the Holy Spirit of God gives you the freedom that will then bring about change and God will tell you who you really are.

Learn to trust God.

You are a
wonderful
idea of God
created for
this time and
hour.

15

YOUR PLACE, MY PLACE = GOD + US = OUR PLACE

"It is important to unite our individualities in marriage because we are no longer two people, but one. This is excellent because there is a stronger connection between us than before. You will enjoy everything together".

Some couples have the habit of saying "this is my place, this is yours." This is one of the issues that not everyone wants to analyze.

Even though your life as a man - whatever it may be - will be different when you get married, you still desire in your heart to continue keeping your friends or work mates.

I worked in the Federal Court for several years. I remember that it was customary to go out to eat with workmates after work.

However, when I met my husband, he also worked in a job similar to mine, but in another dependency. I remember that we just wanted to be together. He used to pick me up and we would have lunch or walk every day. We did not even miss a single opportunity to share moments together. In addition, we had mutual friends in the church where we attended.

We began to do something very intelligent during our first years of marriage. We still kept our friends, but we always went together everywhere and shared our friends. Many couples were formed at that time. Later, they married successfully. It is important to stress that we united our individualities in marriage because we were no longer two people, but one. This was excellent because there was a stronger connection between us.

We enjoyed everything. We shared the same outings, even vacation trips. We joined our individual friendships and attained a bigger group of friends.

I truly believe that when God is in the midst of a man and a woman, unity is unavoidable. Certainly, this is the opposite of what the world offers.

Many failures and infidelities occur as a result of the place and time allowed. When you love a woman and you know that she is your wife, you are going to take care of her and to make her yours in all areas of your life. Both of you will be accountable to each other about the people you were with and what you did. You will do it amicably, without any pressure or annoyance whatsoever.

126

I have mentioned that certain jealousy is healthy. It has to do with the interest in caring for the other, but without being possessive. The possessive person sends messages or makes phone calls several times a day. We often believe that women do this. However, there are very possessive men that are extremely controlling people.

Every man who has these features does not show it at the beginning of a relationship, but it rather emerges over time. I wish to emphasize that when a man does it because he loves his wife, it is because he wants to make her happy. He does not want to see her suffer. Whenever you destroy her self-esteem, you destroy yourself. You must remember that you are one flesh.

My husband and I once counseled a couple where the husband had been unfaithful even though he had an excellent wife.

When we asked him why he had done it, he answered: "I needed someone to understand me." I must confess that his answer surprised and somewhat annoyed us because we thought he was going to tell us that he liked the other woman or because he wanted to have affairs. However, his answer was "I needed someone to understand me".

What happened there? Wasn't his wife understanding? Was she an aggressive or argumentative woman? No, she wasn't! On the contrary, she was a good, sweet and an excellent woman. I would even dare to say that she was a better person than him. The problem was that she had given him too much space.

He did not let her know what he did during the day. She slept late. When she got up she went shopping, met people and he had absolute freedom to do whatever he pleased with his time. He had too much space. Likewise, he was very proud because he earned a lot of money.

What happened then? He had a lover for three years who did whatever she pleased with him. She even managed to have a big control over this man's life.

You take care of what you love. You have to be the center of attention for her and she for you. You must truly and fully trust her and she in you.

This couple has been restored by the powerful work of our Lord and by our work of more than two years counseling and ministering to them.

What was the piece of advice given to them? They had to do absolutely everything together. It was not easy at all. They underwent many difficulties. However, their marriage has been healed by the power of God.

There are men who want everything immediately. If he calls her, she has to answer him at once, or she has to rush in order to assist him. This is arrogance on the part of the man and it should not be so. You must be patient. Otherwise, you will have serious difficulties and fights over time.

I want to share with you that my cell phone and my husband´s cell phone are interconnected. So we have nothing to hide. This is called transparency. If there´s something we do not like, we discuss it through intelligent conversations.

I am deeply grateful to God for my husband's life because he is very intelligent and mature. He is an example to all those who know him. We admire him. He is very wise and loving. He protects every member of our family and church. Thank you, Lord.

Transparency:
Hiding nothing
from each other.

You take care of what you love. You have to be the center of attention for her and she for you. You must truly and fully trust her and she in you.

16

YOUR DOG WELCOMES YOU HAPPILY, BUT YOUR WIFE DOES NOT.

"Self-confident women have a very particular sparkle in their eyes. They always radiate optimism. They laugh at what is to come. They are always happy and in a very good mood. They are never in a bad temper that constantly sets you back".

All our issues are with people, because your dog will neither get mad at you nor make a scene. On the contrary, he is very faithful. You can even push him off your side and whenever you call him back, he comes happily wagging his tail. Doesn´t he?

Men believe that women are like them; that they have the same feelings, that they feel no pain at all, that they are as strong as men are.

That is the big difference between her and your cute pet: feelings.

I would like to ask you the following questions:

1. Do you lose your temper quickly?

2. Are you argumentative?

3. What would your spouse think about it?

I read about a teacher who had given her students an assignment and asked them to complete a sentence that began with the word: "I wish ...", and they had to write what they wanted: a puppy, a toy, a bicycle, etc.

When the teacher corrected the assignments, she was amazed at what many of her students wished for.

> *"I wish my parents did not fight and that my father returned home."*

> *"I wish my mother didn't scream all day."*

> *"I wish I could get good grades so that my father loved me."*

> *"I wish I had only one mother and one father so that the other children did not make fun of me."*

How many people there are that never believe they have a serious problem because they are completely unconcerned about what their children may feel?

The concerned spouse and the unconcerned spouse always exist: the one who keeps hurting with his words and the one who suffers in silence.

The Bible establishes the following: "*The words of the reckless pierce like swords, but the tongue of the wise brings healing*". (Proverbs 12:18.

Offensive words may produce emotional harm that will take a long time to heal. They can even lead to domestic violence.

Getting married is not a harmless act. Notice this verse of the Bible:

> "*But if you do marry, you have not sinned; and if a virgin marries, she has not sinned. But those who marry will face many troubles in this life, and I want to spare you this*". (1° Corinthians 7:28).

> "*But avoid foolish controversies and genealogies and arguments and quarrels about the law, because these are unprofitable and useless*". (Titus 3:9).

Many times we want to express what they deserve because they have really harmed us, but since everyone has their own version of the facts, only time will tell who is right and who is wrong. Do you understand now why your wife sometimes does not greet you happily when you get home? You must also pay attention to how you listen.

The Book of Proverbs 15:28 establishes the following: *"The heart of the righteous weighs its answers, but the mouth of the wicked gushes evil"*.

Proverbs 15:1 adds the following: *"A gentle answer turns away wrath, but a harsh word stirs up anger"*.

Arguments are to be solved and not to be won. Many Biblical verses teach us about the power of words.

> *"Let your conversation be always full of grace, seasoned with salt, so that you may know how to answer everyone"*. (Colossians 4:6.

If you respect the opinion of another person, your own opinion will be respected and taken into account when necessary.

> *"Experience makes you more patient, and you are most patient when you ignore insults"* (Proverbs 19:11, ERV).

Listen to your wife. Get the best out of her.

> *"Sin is not ended by multiplying words, but the prudent hold their tongues"*. (Proverbs 10:19).

> *"Not looking to your own interests but each of you to the interests of the others"*. (Philippians 2:4).

You must always respond to her with affection, even if you find it hard to do.

I think the following biblical text is the most appropriate for the subject in question...

> *"Love is patient, love is kind. It does not envy, it does not boast, it is not proud. It does not dishonor others, it is not self-seeking, it is not easily angered, it keeps no record of wrongs. Love does not delight in evil but rejoices with the truth. It always protects, always trusts, always hopes, always perseveres".* (1 Corinthians 13:4-7).

Self-confident women have a very particular sparkle in their eyes. They always radiate optimism. They laugh at what is to come. They are always happy and in a very good mood. They are never in a bad temper that constantly sets you back.

Arguments are to be solved and not to be won.

Remember how special and particular she is. Encourage and get the best out of her so she can receive you as happily as you have dreamed of. A pleasant and happy woman will pass on her joy to your life.

HE IS A WOMAN WATCHER

17

"God has given you self-discipline. So you have to put it to practice. He helps you, but you must do your part."

I have heard women complain about this on several occasions. Men, unlike women, are more visual. It is commonly said that "men are attracted to physical beauty". I'm sure you have been caught looking at a beautiful woman more than once and your wife made a big fuss.

You thought no one had seen you, but your wife is more insightful than you think. Ah! When she tells you so, you definitely deny it. Somehow you have to escape, don't you?

There is a biblical text whereby Jesus Christ establishes a divine prohibition:

"But I tell you that anyone who looks at a woman lustfully has already committed adultery with her in his heart. If your right eye causes you to stumble, gouge it out and throw it away. It is better for you to lose one part of your body than for your whole body to be thrown into hell". (Matthew 5:28-29).

When a man looks at a woman lustly, he looks at certain parts of her body. This is very dangerous. It is worse if you look at her wishing her sexually, no matter whether she is single or married, but not being your wife.

Your wife is more emotional than you are. What may seem unimportant to you is not to her. She may spend many days thinking about that action of yours of looking at other women. For her it is mentally draining because she always keeps thinking about what you did to her and she imagines worse things: "what will he do when I am not with him?", especially if the other woman is someone you see regularly.

DON'T DO TO OTHERS WHAT YOU WOULD NOT HAVE THEM DO TO YOU.

You have to think that you are demeaning her. She may have fixed herself up for you and you get "distracted" by another woman that passed by. You must understand that all you do is due to immaturity and lack of consideration. She is not only showing jealousy, but she is setting limits and asking you to respect her.

There is a text in the Book of 1 Corinthians 16:13, that commands man the following: *"be courageous; be strong"*. The dictionary definition of "courageous man" is masculine, vigorous, resistant, determined, energetic, strong, brave, firm or virile. It is related to a manly man or that belongs to this type of person.

Therefore, every man must be strong and brave because cowards - as a biblical text also establishes - *"will be consigned to the fiery lake of burning sulfur"*. For this reason, you must be brave.

Those people who find it difficult to make a real change in their lives and habits, those who do not totally trust the Lord and those who savor the things that the world offers and always look back, are those people who Jesus Christ was referring to when he said; *"No one who puts a hand to the plow and looks back is fit for service in the kingdom of God."* (Luke 9:62).

The Bible establishes you are not to do to others what you would not have them do to you.

It is possible that you cannot imagine the damage you have caused her, thus generating a whirlwind of feelings in her. However, there is nothing better than solving the conflict.

Some people act as if nothing ever happened, but it is a way of avoiding the problem. Others find refuge in silence. I advise you to use wisdom and make a real change.

"Blessed are the peacemakers, for they will be called children of God" . (Matthew 5:9).

There are quarrelsome and rebellious people everywhere. There is no doubt that they serve the devil. But the person who is a peacemaker, as God's

Word establishes, is someone who contributes to the well-being of others, has good relationships and especially, he wishes the well-being of his neighbors.

Peacemakers feel good with themselves. They know how to cultivate the art of feeling good with themselves, so they also know how to make other people feel good with them.

Your life must reflect the true character of the Heavenly Father. God is a God of peace. He always wants our well-being.

Your must leave your bad habits behind. You are the only one who knows how to satisfy and bring joy to the person who loves you the most.

God has given you self-discipline. So you have to put it to practice. He will help you, but you must do your part. God bless you.

18

MAN'S INFIDELITY TURNS HIM INTO THE WOMAN'S PUPPET

"You have married to make your spouse happy. Therefore, seeing your spouse happy will complete your happiness".

Women's indifference make married men think and act more out of instinct than out of love and faithfulness. Some of the reasons why men act like this are: the abandonment of her part, primarily in intimacy, lack of sexual desire (sexual intimacy is man's first need), and man's idiosyncrasy: who always needs adventure and exciting relationships.

This does not mean that a man has to be unfaithful. It does not justify him because "the other woman" is available and his wife is exhausted due to excessive work, or simply because she has no sexual desire. But love affairs lead to something beyond sex, and people start feeling affection as the soul remains linked to the other person.

When a man is not close to his wife, he feels guilty and resentful. That period in which they either want to or don´t want to have sexual relations shatters the intimacy of the couple, this is very dangerous. When a man is unfaithful, his wife passes over to have control over everything despite forgiving him and moving on. This situation is really terrible.

SOME MARRIAGES NEED A SECOND HONEYMOON AND TO COME BACK TO GOD'S ORIGINAL PLAN.

I have not read about this topic in any book. My husband and I have personally verified it by helping many married couples on the verge of breakup because men and women stated to have fallen in love with their lovers. Certainly, it was always due to lack of attention by one of them, abandonment and neglect. In short, disinterest and routine had made them reach desperate limits.

It was lack of understanding in both cases. In the case of the man, the problem is in the sexual area because he needs exclusivity in his relationship with his wife; when satisfied, he finds a source of love and pleasure in his wife. But if it is not satisfied, he feels very frustrated.

On the other hand, the woman needs a much more intimate communication with her husband, that involves true feelings.

This makes her surrender herself to the man she loves. This leads her to supply his biggest need: sexual intimacy.

For this reason, I always say that some marriages need a second honeymoon and to come back to God's original plan for marriage because, except for some particular situations, they are both responsible.

This way, love and passion are renewed. When a man and a woman decide to be together, they do not do so because they have an excellent communication or because they solve their conflicts very easily. They decide to marry because they are in love and they find each other person irresistible. This is true and it is what many people tend to lose as time passes.

Man always needs to feel that he draws his wife´s attention, that he is admired and respected. He yearns to be needed by her. Even though the woman is the "weaker vessel", the man is also sensitive and needs to be her priority.

Therefore, you must break that barrier and ask for intimacy so that you will be able to give, but also receive what you need from her.

Everything must be spoken honestly, wisely, with love, so she can understand your needs and desires. Of course, you have to satisfy hers as well.

Both of you must set aside time for each other and stop rushing due to the quick pace of life. Your mutual sincerity is extremely necessary. Silence and shame should be avoided. You must always meet each other's needs because children consume great part of a couple's energy.

I met a beautiful couple in one of our trips to a country in Central America. They had a girl and a baby boy of about six months. It caught my attention how the man felt with his baby. He took care of him and held him in his arms. However, his wife did not look very happy despite the good attitudes of her husband.

She told me that their child had been really desired. However, her marriage was very unstable because of his many infidelities. Thus, she had suffered for many years. In spite of the fact that she was very young, she looked very tired. After attending all the conference meetings they were both renewed, specially him. He really wanted to make a change.

Soon afterwards, she died unexpectedly in a hospital. Today, he really has no words to express how much he misses and needs her.

In most cases, when a man's wife dies, he finds it difficult to move on with his life, with his future. For this reason, it is very important to value and care for the person God has given you.

In order to understand and recognize the good and true values in men and women's lives, you must apply all these principles which will save you from many problems and painful situations. It is useless for me to teach you how to solve conflicts if I cannot convince you that you must avoid doing anything that makes her unhappy.

Life has been given to us by God and we cannot waste it, as others depend on us: wife and children.

Man always needs to feel that he draws his wife's attention, that he is admired and respected.

Remember: you have married to make your spouse happy. Therefore, seeing your spouse happy, will complete your happiness.

NOW... IT IS TIME TO RELINQUISH ALL YOUR VICES

19

"You must experience a moral change so you can recognize, with the light of God, your vices and bad habits, everything that deprives you of your ability to react and keeps you dormant spiritually."

As you begin to mature and be transformed spiritually, you have to give up certain attitudes. God's Word orders that believers must give up lust of the flesh: vanities of life, emptiness, lack of results, disqualifications. Now your spirit must be freed, broken, and restored.

You must experience a moral change so you can recognize, with the light of God, your vices and bad habits, everything that deprives you of your ability to react and keeps you dormant spiritually. Selfishness is also destructive. Immediate satisfaction is long-term destruction.

This reminds me of a case where a wife discovers that her husband, who serves God in the church praise team, watches pornography since his childhood. His father had started this habit in him by giving him illicit magazines.

His father, even as an old man, kept consuming this kind of material.

This is why the Bible establishes that not everything our parents gave us was good. [9] Who was the biggest culprit? ... His own father.

SELFISHNESS IS ALSO DESTRUCTIVE. IMMEDIATE SATISFACTION IS LONG-TERM DESTRUCTION

You must suspect of everything that has to do with the world. It does not offer anything good. All it offers you is distorted. When you observe the magnitudes of your actions, when you become aware of the sins and iniquities in which you find yourself submerged, there God's truth appears and illuminates the dark areas of your soul.

Some people have experienced chaotic disorder in their lives for many years, years of desolation and bitterness. Lonely and confused, they resort to alcohol and drugs, they also lose absolute control of their minds and harm the person who once chose them as husbands. If you are a single father, you must be very wise and not harm the generation that comes after you. This generation is not to blame or responsible for your past life.

Many years ago, a sister's husband who attended church services was an alcoholic and used to get drunk in such a way that he would pass out on the floor of his house for hours. That caused her many problems.

9 Paraphrase of 1 Peter 1:18.

He started attending church services and every time people were called to the altar to accept Jesus Christ as their Savior, he approached the altar, even when there were guest pastors preaching.

I remember that one day he came to our house and asked my husband to help him stop drinking. My husband, who is very objective, told him: "No. I am not going to do what you must do yourself. That is your own determination. It is your will. You must abandon your vice now".

GOD'S POWER THAT BROUGHT HIS BELOVED SON, JESUS CHRIST, BACK TO LIFE, RESURRECTS YOUR LIFE SPOILED BY VICES AND ADDICTIONS.

He never stopped drinking. He left his wife and never returned.

Likewise, another brother who came to church felt the presence of God as soon as he entered the church. He automatically said: "I'll stop drinking, I'll quit because God is real in me".

Today this brother serves in one of the ministry departments and never again drank. What is the difference between them? God helps us, but human beings must do their part.

First of all, the person must be aware of the damage he has been doing to his own body. He must determine the behavior to follow, such as not meeting with those who incite the bad habit, leaving old habits behind and replacing them with new friends, especially Christians.

One day God's Glory is manifested in your life. It is an unmerited favor, a free gift that the Lord pours out on your life. Thus, God's power that brought his beloved son, Jesus Christ, back to life, resurrects your life spoiled by vices and addictions. Glory to God.

A very famous actor born in England is today an alcoholic because his father instilled this bad habit in him. Despite his fame and money, no wife remains by his side because nothing can stop his addiction.

You must seek your true Father who has created and formed you, who has given you a new opportunity. You must also get to know God more and more. Likewise, you have to establish new relationships that keep you away from bad environments.

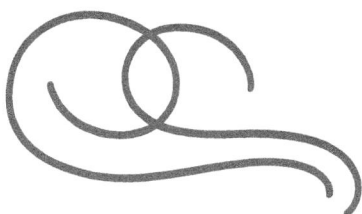

Ask the Holy Spirit
of God to fill you.
The Bible states:
"Do not get drunk on
wine, which leads to
debauchery. Instead,
be filled with
the Spirit."
(Ephesians 5:18).

20

THE SOLUTION FOR YOUR LACK OF LOVE

"God's love is perfected in us. Therefore, we must perfect ourselves in his love because many people will lose their faith and it will be replaced by sight. Hope will turn into hopelessness, but God's love is eternal. It never fails".

When we accept Jesus Christ as our Savior and He fills all areas of our life: body, soul and spirit, God's love - according to his Word - will be poured out in our hearts.

The expression "poured out" gives the idea of abundance, according to John 10:10. For that reason, you must ask yourself: "What am I doing with the superabundant love that God pours into my life?

One morning I woke up and God told me that His love was perfected in us. I started doing research and I found so many biblical texts about this topic that I was really amazed.

"But if anyone obeys his word, love for God is truly made complete in them. This is how we know we are in him" (1 John 2:5).

God's love is perfected in the person who obeys his Word.

God has an individual plan for every one of us. Now, it is up to us for that plan to come to completion. This occurs as long as we obey the Holy Spirit of God and his Word.

Some people say: "I ran out of love".

Our beloved Savior, Jesus Christ, is not like people who reject or hurt us. He loves us everlastingly. For this reason, we must perfect ourselves in his love because many people will lose their faith and it will be replaced by sight. Hope will turn into hopelessness, but God's love is eternal. It never ends.

I want to paraphrase about love as the basis of all gifts.

Each synonym that appears in the Book of 1 Corinthians, Chapter 13 have tremendous depth, because through love the best gifts are manifested in our lives.

Love is protector. It is patient. Love is kind.

It is natural that it does us good.

Love does not envy. So it is not competitive. It does not boast, that is, it does not live off of appearances. It is not proud, that is, it is courteous. It does not dishonor others; on the contrary, it seeks the well-being of others. It is not self-seeking, it is rather pleased with the rights of others. It is not easily angered, it maintains a peaceful attitude. It keeps no record of wrongs, that is, you do not take into account how many times you have been hurt. Love does not delight in evil, but rejoices with the truth. Love always protects, always trusts, always hopes, always perseveres. It is always faithful. Love never fails. [10]

God´s Word establishes in the Book of 2 Corinthians 5:14 that God´s love "compels" us, that is, it surrounds us completely. You cannot stop feeling it.

It surrounds you completely. How wonderful! We have no option other than to receive that love, because He is love. We cannot just say that God loves, God is love. His love modifies all aspects of our life. The man who loves God must love people in all his relationships: as husband, as father, as son and as a Christian. He must also allow God to perfect the love in him. The Book of Colossians 3:14 establishes the following: *"And over all these virtues put on love, which binds them all together in perfect unity"*.

---

10 See 1 Corinthians 13:4-8.

When we are mentally structured, we prevent God from perfecting the love in us. Many people do not really know what love is and only regard it as a feeling. You have to see the essence of everything and God 's essence is love. As I have previously expressed, He is love. It is his essence.

You need more than feelings to sustain a relationship. Many men do not know about this, because they need to have knowledge about it. The idea of learning about love may seem a joke to some people who are reading this. Indeed, you have learned from television and stories where feelings such as love, hate, guilt, betrayal or revenge abound. However, real life is not like that, it is not a novel.

You minister to your wife's needs through love. This is why God perfects the love in you so you are not a slave of your feelings, but so that you may choose to perform acts of love, because it is your decision. The following is my last reflection:

You must choose love and let God perfect it in you. Thus, you are obeying His Word.

The man who decides to be a conqueror prepares himself intellectually and spiritually.

21

MAN IS A NATURAL-BORN CONQUEROR

"A conqueror acts according to his faith because he walks towards his purpose without knowing, many times, the end of his conquest ".

This chapter is aimed at the mature man with years of experience in life.

Maybe you have been defeated many times during your life. However, something inside yourself motivates you to be a conqueror. This is why it bothers you when people think you cannot achieve it because you have the ability to complete what you have decided to do.

A conqueror ...

- Is a man who acts according to his faith because he walks towards his purpose without knowing, many times, the end of his conquest.

- Values the true character of people.

- Is guided by the principles established in God's Word.

- Acts prudently and not impulsively. He takes his time and evaluates everything.

- Knows to wait for the right time and prepares himself.

- Is extremely responsible and discreet in his work.

- Does not disclose his personal affairs, he keeps secret and is trustworthy.

- Allows his wife to grow in all areas of her life.

My daughter, Damaris, is married to a young Italian man. Their story is marvelous because she met Domenico, her husband, in the same small town in Italy where my paternal grandfather was born. Since they got married, they have grown up together and he has allowed her to grow in all areas of her life.

Today my daughter is an excellent pastor in our ministry, but her husband also preaches to the youth. They are an exemplary marriage to all those who know them. They are working very hard and are pleased to be continually molded by my husband and myself: their parents and counselors.

He understands that together they will be truly blessed. However, they also decide to conquer something new every day. They spend time daily doing business and working together. This is very important because the Bible establishes the following "... But **woe to him who is alone** when he falls and does not have another to lift him up". [11]

Domenico always consults everything with her because he understands that our daughter has a position of spiritual authority delegated by her father, my husband, and because she has a longer life as a Christian than him. He is determined to be a conqueror in the United States of America.

The man who decides to be a conqueror prepares himself intellectually and spiritually. He can talk about any topic. He analyzes what he is going to say in detail and is very objective. He knows what he wants very well. He expects to be successful, even though it may take him a few years to accomplish it.

YOU HAVE THE ABILITY TO COMPLETE WHAT YOU HAVE DECIDED TO DO.

I want to give an example based on the biblical story about Caleb. One day Caleb and Joshua, his companion, had to explore the promised land of Israel:

"...Joshua son of Nun and Caleb son of Jephunneh, who were among those who had explored the land, tore their clothes and

---

11 Ecclesiastes 4:10.

> *said to the entire Israelite assembly,*
> *"The land we passed through and*
> *explored is exceedingly good. If the Lord is*
> *pleased with us, he will lead us into that*
> *land, a land flowing with milk and honey,*
> *and will give it to us. Only do not rebel*
> *against the Lord. And do not be afraid of*
> *the people of the land, because we will*
> *devour them. Their protection is gone, but*
> *the Lord is with us. Do not be afraid*
> *of them."* (Numbers 14:6-9).

So, they came to Moses giving good news: "we are going to conquer that land. We can do it." The other ten spies concluded with fear that it could not be conquered. God Himself promised to bless Caleb by giving him the promised land because of his faith. Caleb neither minimized the giants on earth nor the fortified cities he saw, but He glorified God's power.

> *"So Joshua blessed Caleb and gave him*
> *Hebron as a permanent inheritance*
> *because he had followed the Lord God of*
> *Israel".* (Joshua 14:14, TLB Living Bible).

However, Caleb waited for 45 years to inherit the land he had explored with Joshua. They spent difficult years traveling throughout the desert. However, this conqueror fully trusted in God's promises.

Caleb was 85 years old at the end of the conquest. He was as strong as he was when he was 45.

"I am as strong now as I was when Moses sent us on that journey, and I can still travel and fight as well as I could then!" (Joshua 14:11).

The most extraordinary event was Caleb's conquest of the promised land because the land was freed from war. Do you still want to conquer something in your life? Glorify God´s power.

Hebron, the best piece of land, was given to this great conqueror, Caleb. Then his inheritance increased. This is because we serve a Powerful God. His blessings enrich us and motivate us to achieve big conquests.

Does time matter? No, it doesn´t matter when you are a visionary. Don't let old age turn yourself into a man who complains about everything. God still has many things to give you. As long as you are alive, God continues working.

Faith and perseverance were the source of Caleb´s success. He was the conqueror. The same giants that the other ten spies feared were the ones that Caleb expelled from Hebron. Later, that land became his inheritance because God had promised it to him.

One day God told my husband and I, when our three children were still very young, that they would be freed from big dangers. Now they are older, but I still claim that promise from God and He fulfills it. His presence will strengthen you and will make you rest.

"Those who are victorious will inherit all these things...." (Revelation 21:7).

All means all.

You must defeat the enemy as Caleb did and take possession of your inheritance, persevere and believe in God's promises. Keep your mind and heart fixed on the inheritance.

Only God will make you victorious. Amen.

You have the
ability to finish
doing what you
set out to do.

God's promises are always fulfilled. Take possession of your victory in faith.

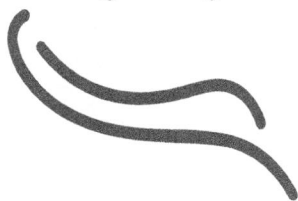

MAN AND HIS INHERITANCE

22

*"God loves blessing people, but he is a God
that blesses for generations.
In other words, if God finds a man who is
willing to follow him, it is a guarantee that
his offspring will be prosperous."*

The absence of passionate men of God in the church has an impact on the next generation. Children who later become teenagers and do not attend church anymore because their father does not attend are a clear example of this.

If you are a servant of God, why don't you look for what the heavenly Father has already prepared for you?

The enemy has worked very hard to prevent you from receiving your inheritance. Yes, it is an inheritance that God has entrusted to you, and the enemy does not want you to receive it.

God is the God of Abraham, Isaac and Jacob.

God loves blessing people but he is a God that blesses for generations. In other words, if God finds a man who is willing to follow him, it is a guarantee that his offspring will be prosperous.

God does not have any problem with abundance. God does not add, He is a God who multiplies. The Bible establishes in the Book of Matthew 25:29 (NLT *"To those who use well what they are given, even more will be given, and they will have an abundance..."*

God operates by the generosity of his grace.

The good use of gifts and talents given by God will make you progress and produce good works. Grace is God's favor. It is an undeserved gift. God loves blessing us.

The Book of Psalm 127:3 establishes the following:" *"Children are an heritage of the LORD..."*. (KJV.

It is important for a man of courage to appreciate his children because they are his inheritance, his offspring. A man honors God by taking care of his inheritance because he establishes domain on earth. God gives children to men like a fortune to heirs. It is true that children are born bringing a blessing.

Our last grandson, Liam, is our son´s and daughter-in-law´s son. He was born when they had just bought their own house. Before our first grandchild, Ethan, was born, my son had found an excellent job that allowed him to start a career and graduate as a Notary Public.

Children do not always listen to parents, but they always imitate them. They never forget their example. Therefore, your children must follow you in the same way as you follow Christ. God will give spiritual children to those people who do not have natural children.

A true man assumes the responsibility throughout his life to love and sacrifice himself for the next generation, caring for them, honoring God and guiding them to obey the Lord. They are his inheritance.

I vividly remember a brother named Francisco. Every Sunday he would pick me up and take me to church since I was four years old. I also remember an Italian man named Donato. He was the person who prayed more fervently at the moment of receiving Holy Communion during church services. Likewise, I

remember an excellent teacher, Mr. Abel, an expert in God's Word. I remember many other servants of God who have been an example for my life.

GOD OPERATES BY THE GENEROSITY OF HIS GRACE.

As a young woman I have also seen my husband grow spiritually as he was always serving God in the church where we used to attend. I have seen him grow when God called both of us to serve him.

He is my beloved husband. He is very radical, hardworking, brave and determined to serve God.

What do I mean? The role of a man is very important for the following generations to love and serve the Lord.

Once again, God wants to work through man.

Every man is a promise. The man who loves God will have a new identity, moral values and will be committed in everything he does. His life will be an inexhaustible source because he will have a spiritual life that will bring balance to his family. His past life does not matter because the Lord makes "all things new".

Material progress can neither replace the spiritual, nor make man's dreams come true because feelings of emptiness will always arise and only God can fill such void.

Greg Laurie, pastor and evangelist, in the New Believer's Bible, identified the problem that human beings face: *"We all have a hole in our heart, a spiritual emptiness deep inside our souls, a 'blank space' which has the shape of God "*.

For that reason, God wants you to enter his rest. What does it mean? It means calmness, confidence, strength. It means to enjoy more and to do less. It means that others work for you. Ah! That is really good, isn't it? But I mean to create a family-owned company or business managed by your own sons or daughters, or where trustworthy people you have trained or prepared, work for you. Thus, you become the source of income for them. This is extraordinary.

Some people have had bad experiences at working with Christians, whether with Christian employees or bosses. However, I wonder, how is it possible this happens, when, unlike unbelievers, they are supposed to believe in Jesus Christ?

There are carnal Christians and spiritual Christians. I can affirm this after many years of experience in ministering to people. Here is where you need to have discernment to choose the right people and be a man of character.

WHEN YOU ENTER GOD'S REST YOU MAKE TIME COUNT MORE THAN EVER BEFORE.

Work is very important and you have to take care of it. You must . not play with employees. I remember that my husband would always tell a brother: "don't play with your employees because they will never respect you". And so it was: they never respected and even criticized him.

When you enter God's rest, you make time count more than ever before and you can even visit places you have always dreamed of visiting. However, when the Lord prospers you, you must not be proud and miserly, you have to always recognize that everything comes from Him.

You must also match the highly valued virtues of your present time with the best of the past. We usually affirm that "the past was better." However, it is good to live day by day.

I believe that the information technology era we are living today is much more advantageous because it allows us to do what Jesus Christ said in the Book of John

EVERY MAN MUST DEVELOP ALL AREAS OF HIS LIFE.

14:12 *"whoever believes in me will do the works I have been doing, and they will do even greater things than these..."* precisely due to the global reach of the internet and globalization.

Therefore, the church needs men committed to love as Jesus Christ did. He is the best model for us. For that reason, every man must get to know Him.

Every man must develop all areas of his life. If you are faithful to God you will be trusted by people and you will no longer have to conceal your identity. On the contrary, everyone must see that you shine, that someone different dares to reveal to the world that everything is possible with Jesus Christ.

You can be better than your father, grandfather, or great-grandfather. You must show that, from you on, a thousand generations will receive God's blessings because you are a true believer.

"Know therefore that the Lord your God is God; he is the faithful God, keeping his covenant of love to a thousand generations of those who love him and keep his commandments". (Deuteronomy 7:9).

You must bring up and discipline them because you love them and want the best for them.

God wants to establish a holy offspring through you, as children require a prudent stewardship so they can obey the Lord. Everything you do for God's work will bless your generations.

*Every man
is a
promise.*

Seek the Lord,
"being confident of
this, that he who
began a good work in
you will carry it on to
completion until the
day of Christ Jesus"
(Philippians 1:6)

23

DISCOVER YOUR PURPOSE IN LIFE

"If you go from a negative to a positive state of mind, you become a lively man and resemble a magnet. People wish to be with you because your mind is the most important creative fuel for the fulfillment of your purpose".

There is something that only you can do in your life.

Of course, we all know someone who has inspired and guided us. However, you must discover the main gift that will really satisfy you in everything you undertake.

Every person is the result of the people they have been influenced by, the environment where they have been educated and the place where they spend most of the time. Whoever works in an office where people gossip, they will also gossip. Those people who spend time in a bar with drunkards will also become alcoholics. If you work on the road with fellow jokers and mockers, you will go home and will make fun of your wife and children. The following famous saying is real: "Birds of a feather flock together".

God's Word establishes that Jesus does everything new if you come to him. That is wonderful!

He fills your life with love. God loves you so much that you have to love others as well. His peace invades you, that peace that neither the world nor anyone else could offer you. He enters your spirit and creates in you a "new creation". The Lord has to renew your mind, because if He changes your thoughts, He will also change your life. [12] You are a new man; those people who know you can assure you have really changed.

Many people are ignorant about spirituality, especially those who have accepted Jesus Christ as their personal Savior. Many people live as they wish, not obeying God´s Word, and thinking that they are true believers and that God has to bless them.

The apostle Paul urges us to take care of our spiritual life, especially salvation, in many of his epistles. I want you to know that God´s work truly transforms our lives. It is His divine intervention, and not our work, because everything in the Christian life is God's work.

Now, you are expected to make a real change.

---

12 See Romans 12:2.

You must no longer live according to your own thoughts, but according to God´s Word. Your eternal life is at stake.

Man needs a model, a counselor, a spiritual leader to help him find his true purpose.

I also hope this book is of value to you. I have read many books which have really helped me. It is said that women read more books than men. However, I know this book is different and that you are enjoying reading it.

Now, your purpose will depend on how much you honor those who have taught you. God loves to bless those who move towards the completion of His promises.

GOD'S WORK TRULY TRANSFORMS OUR LIVES

First, I want to teach you that God's commandments will support us in our purpose. It has to do with honoring our parents, who may also be spiritual parents, in the case your natural parents have passed away.

It is a command that contains a promise. But it is more effective when you do it with material things.

My mother is the only person who is still alive in my family. Every month we send her a monetary offering which does not only help her, but also the following biblical verse is fulfilled:

"Honor your father and mother"-which is the first commandment with a promise- "so that it may go well with you and that you may enjoy long life on the earth." (Ephesians 6:2-3).

What will happen then?

Everything you undertake will go well and you will enjoy long life. Your life will be useful and will have a purpose. God gave this commandment with promise to Moses, but the Apostle Paul made it more abundant in the New Testament.

I have personally seen this promise come true because the established blessing has always prospered us and has also opened doors for us to preach all over the world.

EVERYTHING THAT IS IN LINE WITH GOD'S DESIRE FOR YOU, CAN BE ACHIEVED.

We have built churches in the United States of America, the European Union, Central America, Nigeria, an annex of our Christian University and we continue moving forward and growing.

We are a model and testimony to many people, as a family, as a married couple and individually; in my case before women, and in the case of my husband, before men.

We come from an environment where we have always dressed well, with a lot or little resources to clothes, but it is part of our essence and people imitate us. Today our ministry is a ministry of excellence because we serve an excellent God.

As far as I am concerned, we must give the best to God. That doesn't prevent you from being humble.

Humble is the person who learns how to treasure everything that God has given him, values others and respects them, and does not exercise dominion over his fellow man.

I think there is a false humbleness: the poorer I look, the more spiritual I am. This is not true. It is a complete lie.

The Book of Ecclesiastes 9:15 establishes the following: *"But nobody remembered that poor man ..."* It is true, isn´t it? It speaks about the spiritual poor and gives no examples.

Everything that is in line with God's desire for you, can be achieved. But you must have a clear vision of your future.

You must establish short and long term goals. My husband always asks me: "What are you thinking?", because the mind is the most important creative fuel for the fulfillment of your purpose. When the mind is renewed by the Spirit of God, it is more perceptive to the coming opportunities.

In short, "you spend all day thinking ...", you have a quick mind and dream of a better life. You become a super positive man and you take action, because your mind has gone from a negative to a positive state. You have become a lively man and resemble a magnet. People wish to be with you. You are so wise that your children will ask you for advice and not for their friends´ advice.

Your conversations will be extremely interesting because your life is important, surprising and intense. You will express your gratitude to God for being alive every day because you have learned to capture your opportunity and your moment of glory.

People from Puerto Rico - and I know many people who live there as several singers have visited our ministry — say the following: "It is better to be busy
than worried." This is very good, isn't it?

Anxiety, lack of purpose and disorientation make you go round and round mindlessly. You do everything, but in the end you get nothing from everything you did. However, when God's calling is heard, understood and obeyed, the true purpose for your life is really fulfilled.

If God's Word establishes that "we are more than conquerors," we must trust it. God tells you: "Look, believe it, you are more than that." Hallelujah. You must believe in God, but also in yourself. Many men live, die and fight for total nonsense.

How would you like to be remembered?

I will give the example of my maternal grandfather and my paternal grandfather.

My maternal grandfather was very bad tempered. I recall him as someone who was always angry. If someone stared at him on the bus, he would say: "Hey, why are you looking at me? Do I owe you anything?" We were all afraid of him. When he took a nap in the afternoon, we couldn't make any noise; otherwise, he would get up in a very bad mood and scold us all.

My grandmother's relatives did not have contact with her because my grandfather was so selfish that he didn't want to share her with anyone. Even though he had many brothers, he did not relate to them. He was very lazy, he would only work a couple of hours a day and his house had been built by his brother-in-law. Otherwise, he would have had nothing.

I will never forget the day he got mad at me. He made me cry so much, I was a teenager, and I was very sad for several days. My mother will never forget that my grandfather never allowed her to study. This was very frustrating for her because she is a woman with many gifts and abilities. Needless to say, he was not a Christian and he rejected the gospel on many occasions.

However, when I recall my paternal grandfather, I smile and thank God for his life. He introduced the gospel to us. He had accepted Jesus Christ as his Savior even though he came from a very religious family. He and his brother-in-law were the first two believers in the family.

He was an Italian immigrant and came to Argentina in the 1930s. He lived in a board and lodging. My grandmother had to stay in Italy until he could find a place to live in Argentina.

She stayed in Italy with two children who later died because it was the postwar period and severe famine had spread throughout the country. My grandmother used to tell us that she had worked for a whole year in Italy just to buy a skirt. It sounds terrible, doesn´t it? However, when she arrived in Argentina, the Lord blessed them with two daughters and a son: my father.

My grandfather loved God´s Word. He read the Bible from cover to cover three times. Furthermore, he had dictionaries and biblical commentaries to help him because he hadn´t had the chance to attend school. However, he learned how to read from the Scriptures.

In addition, he helped build several churches in the capital, Buenos Aires. He was always an advamced man for his time. He had learned plumbing in the city where he had lived and had a lot of work. He was the only one who had a telephone in his neighborhood. He was so prosperous that he left a house for each of his three children when he died. His children also inherited two farms on the outskirts of Buenos Aires. He and my grandmother got food for their children and grandchildren from those two farms.

My maternal grandfather left nothing. No one recalls him. However, my paternal grandfather is still recalled in the family as a pioneer, a forerunner and, especially, a servant of God, who left us a spiritual legacy.

Ah! I inherited his Bible and his books. I was the only one in my father's family who responded to God's calling together with my husband. Therefore, ask yourself:

How would you like to be remembered? Like someone who nobody recalls? Or, like a man who has good principles, faith, a man of his word that achieved what he set out to do? Think about it.

24

YOU MUST DETERMINE THE PERSON YOU WISH TO BECOME

"God has given you self-control which is a fruit of the Holy Spirit inside you. It is a spiritual ability. It means to control your emotions, impulses and desire to overeat. It also means to control your sexual needs. It is the ability to control the uncontrollable".

It´s fantastic to go to the doctor´s for a checkup and have them tell you: "Sir, you are completely healthy. All your tests are perfect." This is true, isn´t it?

Have you thought about the importance of your health? I am not writing this chapter to lecture you. According to statistics women are the ones who regularly go to the doctor´s, but you have to be healthy for your own benefit and for those who love you and depend on you.

"… Rather, in humility value others above yourselves…" (Philippians 2:3).

Now that you have understood how important love is and everything related to a woman, children and dreams, it is time to understand how important it is to give up bad eating habits and the sedentary lifestyle, out of love for yourself. You are carrying a heavy burden (whether it is being overweight, stress, concern) and it is time to relinquish them.

You must not allow people to continue calling you "fat" because you are obese, or "skinny" because you have no muscle in your body. Both extremes are bad. There must be an ideal for you, and you have to achieve it.

No matter whether it is genetics or a disorder in the food you eat, you must understand that your health, your quality of life and also your future are at stake. As you grow older, your strength and the desire to do physical exercise will not be the same. Therefore, ask yourself if it is time to start now.

Intimate relations in the order established by God

Married men have very good health and live many years according to research carried out. This is due to emotional stability, for having someone to share life with and, of course, because if they have an active and frequent sexual life, this will benefit both spouses´ health.

This is why the Bible establishes: *"… and may you rejoice in the wife of your youth.* (Proverbs 5:18).

I want to transcribe a teaching taken from "Plenitude" Bible, section: "Kingdom Dynamics" (1 Corinthians 7: 3-4). I think it is one of the best Bibles that teaches about three aspects of sex:

> Unity, symbol of love, reserved for marriage, FAMILY ORDER. Coitus is an intimate expression of affection between husband and wife. The apostle emphasizes the importance of marriage by declaring that sexual act is, indeed, a duty; both husband and wife must be willing and available to each others sexual needs.
>
> It is more than an act of biological mating. The Bible calls it a "mystery," a privilege by which two people: a man and a woman become one (Ephesians 5:32; see Genesis 2:24). That privilege is abused when the man and the woman are not married and have sexual contact (see 1 Corinthians 5:1; 6:16). Therefore, something that should bless us according to God´s purpose becomes a cause for judgment (see Ephesians 5: 5).
>
> Marriage is the only place that God has provided for sexual union to occur.

This intimate act becomes a powerful symbol of the love between Christ and the Church. A sharing of joy and delight between both spouses, a true gift given by God. That outside of these limits it is virtually destructive. (Hosea 2:16, 17, 19, 20 / Isaiah 54: 5) L.C.

There are many misconceptions about sex. I want to teach you a correct and biblical view. The following benefits are the result of having a proper sex life within the framework of marriage:

- It reduces your stress.

- It improves your mood and emotions.

- It strengthens your immune system.

- It is an instant cure for mild depression.

- It makes endorphin circulate through the bloodstream, producing a pleasant feeling of euphoria and well-being.

- The body releases the love hormone (oxytocin) which acts as a natural sedative and unleashes positive emotions.

- If practiced regularly, it improves mental health considerably.

- It brings out emotions, even laughter.

- It becomes less stressful the more often it is practiced. [13]

You will succeed in whatever helps you trust yourself because it will break with your cowardice, your doubts and your fears. What you cannot achieve with your own strength, with God you will achieve it. God has given you self-control which is a fruit of the Holy Spirit inside you. It is a spiritual ability. It means to control your emotions, impulses and desire to overeat. It also means to control your sexual needs. It is the ability to control the uncontrollable.

Of course, in order to achieve this, you must discard everything that is harmful for yourself: habits, movies, friendships, programs, relationships that lead you to waste your time and money.

You will succeed in all this if you have a firm conviction that you wish to receive the rewards for the changes you are determined to do, faith in God´s Word that reveals the truth to you in all areas of your life, especially prayer, and the desire to be transformed.

---

13   Online Consultation : https://www.cnn.com/2018/03/01/health/health-benefits-of-sex-parallels/ index.html

Imagine feeling healthy, looking attractive and your life balanced. You will make an effort and recover your dignity, because now, when people look at you, you will feel different. It is wonderful to be admired.

Your discipline will then take you to celebrate the battles you have won, because you will speak well of yourself. If you do this, you will honor your Creator. You can achieve it.

25

TO THE YOUTH...
WHO CLIMB TO
THE SUMMIT

"The line of your life, young man, has a summit ahead that you must climb".

It is impossible for me not to write to young men because they have a big potential to develop if they obey God, especially when you put in practice God´s commandments since a very early age. This is something you must choose. It is neither very difficult nor impossible.

Life causes disappointments which harden hearts and feelings through the years. The earlier you establish a relationship with God, the better the results you will obtain in life.

I want you to see the line of your life as a summit that you must climb. Each step will take you to reach a goal, a purpose.

There is a story about five young men that were very busy with their lives, studies and jobs. They reached an agreement: to train during a year and save up money to buy luggage and climb a high mountain with ice.

They asked for permission in their jobs and in their studies a year ahead of time. They made the arrangements with their families and trained very hard every week because their goal was to reach the summit. The day of the feat came. They left behind their studies, jobs, families, friends and city.

THE EARLIER YOU ESTABLISH A RELATIONSHIP WITH GOD, THE BETTER THE RESULTS YOU WILL OBTAIN IN LIFE.

They started their journey with all the equipment for which they had invested during that year. They were very happy, euphoric and felt a rush of adrenalin. They arrived at the scene, prepared their luggage and started climbing. It was very cold and windy. However, they had a very clear goal: to reach the summit.

After having climbed for about seven days, they were extremely tired and hungry. They had to face very bad weather conditions such as strong wind, cold and snow. Suddenly, everyone began to smell burning wood and songs seemed to be heard at the distance.

As they continued climbing, they came to a hill and could see a cabin from which smoke was coming out of its chimney. They could also hear singing voices and a delicious smell of chocolate. They immediately started heading to the cabin. They were just halfway through the summit.

After leaving their luggage at the door, they entered and found a cozy, heated place, with food and hot chocolate. After having sung and talked for five hours, some of them said it was time to continue their journey. Three of these young people decided to stay in the cabin and not continue climbing the cold, icy, rainy and snowy path to reach the summit.

So, two of them set out on their journey. As they were climbing, the three young men who had stayed in the cabin constantly looked out of the window at those who continued climbing. As these two got closer to the summit, the joy and excitement of those who had stayed in the cabin disappeared.

When these two young men reached the summit, there was a deadly silence in the cabin. Those who had stayed behind regretted not having made an effort at what they had prepared and invested money during a year.

They realized that they had lost their opportunity, considering they were so close to the goal: the summit.

What is your goal in life?

Motivation and inspiration will be your key to your personal growth and to get you out of comfort. So that you will not feel frustrated like those who stayed in the cabin being so close to achieve their goal and savor the victory of having reached the summit.

Studying, training and equipping yourself will provide you with the tools you need to develop in the area you are good at. Motivation is the spark that starts the engine in your mind to have projects and dreams.

The skills that are perfected when you seek God bring out the treasure inside of you. These skills impart a high level of enthusiasm in you and break away the fear, which is worse than failure. But since you are young, you need to be promoted by someone who is more mature than you and can help you. Find a mentor.

Wisdom wants to be your companion and your helper. Read this biblical text carefully:

> *"And how happy I was with what he created-his wide world and all his family of mankind! And so, young men, listen to me, for how happy are all who follow my instructions.*
> *Listen to my counsel -oh, don't refuse it- and be wise. Happy is the man who is so anxious to be with me that he watches for me daily at my gates, or waits for me outside my home!*

For whoever finds me finds life and wins approval from the Lord. But the one who misses me has injured himself irreparably. Those who refuse me show that they love death." (Proverbs 8:31-36, TLB).

- Let divine wisdom shape your life.

- Treasure spiritual values which will make you reach your goal.

- You have to be disciplined and obedient to receive advice.

- Receive every instruction with joy.

- Learn how to use time wisely. Time is gold and it never comes back.

- Be diligent in your work.

- Use your energies correctly.

- Don't keep away from the truth.

- Don't be proud. Be humble.

- Take special care of your relationship with the Lord.

God's
blessings
will reach
you.

26

EVERY STORY IS BEAUTIFUL, BUT OURS IS MY FAVORITE ONE

One day, early in the morning, God spoke to me about the meaning of the covenant in marriage and our relationship with Jesus Christ.

For example, my husband and I take care of each other 24 hours a day.

Even though we might not be physically in the same place, we have our mind set on the other all the time. I never stop thinking of him. Everything we do, we do thinking in terms of us together.

He is my life, because we are one. It wouldn't even occur to us to hurt one another. We talk and communicate a lot. We share the same tastes.

When I cook, I prepare the menu thinking about the food my husband likes.

When I choose a clothing to wear, I choose what he likes me to wear. When he suggests something related to my make-up, I listen to him and I make the necessary changes to look better.

My life is centered around him. Why? Because we are one and because we live in a relationship of covenant and commitment.

> *"Husbands, love your wives, just as Christ loved the church and gave himself up for her. In this same way, husbands ought to love their wives as their own bodies. He who loves his wife loves himself. After all, no one ever hated their own body, but they feed and care for their body, just as Christ does the church- for we are members of his body. "For this reason, a man will leave his father and mother and be united to his wife, and the two will become one flesh." This is a profound mystery-but I am talking about Christ and the church".* (Ephesians 5:25, 28-32).

Two important things: the two will become one flesh and this is a profound mystery, making reference to Christ and the Church. The marriage covenant is compared to Christ's covenant with the Church. It is essential to have intimacy, permanence, agreement and commitment with Jesus Christ. The same has to happen in our marriage, an intimate and permanent relationship of covenant and commitment. Thus, God speaks to us through his Holy Spirit and we start to get to know him intimately. That is extraordinary.

We have everything with Jesus Christ and we have nothing without him.

I like to say that God has not finished with our lives´ purpose yet. There are still activities in God's calendar where our names appear.

After having looked inside oneself and found the true identity, one has to look ahead. God has drawn the line of our life from eternity to eternity.

This is why the devil has tried by all means to disrupt God's plans for each of us. But he has not been able to.

**God protects us from everything...
even from ourselves.**

It is said that men do not cry. But that is not true.

Tears are liquid prayer. There so great joy when the enemy is defeated by the action of your tears because your tears are a demonstration that you have humbled yourself before the Lord and said: "Lord, I need you."

The most difficult thing is to face our weaknesses; the things we did not want to say but we said; the things we should not have done but we did. I am writing this with tears running down my cheeks just because I think that we all need God to protect us from ourselves.

We must ask the Lord to free us from pride and transform us into humble people. The humble person recognizes he depends on God entirely. He learns to value others and does not intend to control his fellow man. He does not demand anything and gives up his rights for the love to other people. Remember that we are debtors of God's love. We find the most important example of humbleness, of course, in our Lord, Jesus Christ. I love this text with all my heart:

> *"In your relationships with one another, have the same mindset as Christ Jesus: Who, being in very nature God, did not consider equality with God something to be used to his own advantage; rather, he made himself nothing by taking the very nature of a servant, being made in human likeness. And being found in appearance as a man, he humbled himself by becoming obedient to death— even death on a cross! Therefore God exalted him to the highest place and gave him the name that is above every name, that at the name of Jesus every knee should bow, in heaven and on earth and under the earth, and every tongue acknowledge that Jesus Christ is Lord, to the glory of God the Father"*. (Philippians 2:5-11, NIV)

Therefore, you must learn and modify your ideas with God's Word and your best example: Jesus Christ.

"This is what the Lord says: "Let not the wise boast of their wisdom or the strong boast of their strength or the rich boast of their riches, but let the one who boasts boast about this: that they have the understanding to know me, that I am the Lord, who exercises kindness, justice and righteousness on earth, for in these I delight," declares the Lord". (Jeremiah 9:23-24).

Getting to know GOD is to have an intimate relationship with Him, to be connected to the Holy Spirit and to pray in the spirit.

Why don't people pray? Because they lack God´s presence.

Why do people say that God does not speak to them? Because they do not read the Bible. God speaks to us in many ways: One of them is through his Word.

You must avoid distraction because it prevents you from having a specific time to be with God. You look to grow more and more in all areas of your life, but especially in your spiritual life.

DON'T LET BLESSINGS BE FAR FROM YOU.

Sorrow, temptation and disappointment come from people who keep you away from everything that has to do with your soul and your spirit which belong to God.

This is why it is very important to spend some time alone with the Lord.

Because there, under your pain, very hidden, are your deepest secrets, which only God can know and heal.

You will no longer feel pain, sorrow and bitterness. There are many blessings and joys waiting for you. Don't let these blessings escape you. The Bible establishes: "He loved to pronounce a curse— may it come back on him. He found no pleasure in blessing— may it be far from him (Psalm 109:17).

I repeat: don't let blessings be far from you. Cry out to God and He will respond to you. He will fight in your favor. He will not abandon you. He always watches over your soul.

God offers us his Word. His commandments are delightful, attractive and desirable. Every day you have an opportunity to start over. It is never too late to make a change. A lovely verse of the Bible establishes the following:

> *"The Lord your God is with you, the Mighty Warrior who saves. He will take great delight in you; in his love he will no longer rebuke you, but will rejoice over you with singing."* (Zephaniah 3:17).

How extraordinary it is to know that for every unfulfilled dream and for each thing we have loved and lost God has already drawn up a new plan. Therefore, every time the devil intends to stop you, remind him of his end: the fiery lake of burning sulfur, and of our destiny: to reign with Christ on earth and for eternity.

You must fulfill God's eternal purpose for your life. Knowing Christ is everything, and He is God's everything. Remember: nothing is more important than this.

Christ must be shown through your life. "I no longer live, but Christ lives in me" [14].

Christ must be your priority in life. He is everything.

14 Galatians 2:20.

The skills that are perfected when you seek God, bring out the treasure in you.

Christ is our balsam for the moments of greatest need. He is marvelous. He is the wisdom you need to understand your wife and to become the true man to the stature of the Perfect Man: Jesus. He is the unconditional Love with whom you learn to give and receive love because He loves us endlessly. He is the way and the truth and the life. He is our healer. He has chosen us. He restores your life with His power. Amen.

FINAL WORDS

I would like to express my gratitude to you for letting me transmit you more wisdom so you can understand your purpose and vocation. From now on, it is my desire that you can make the most important changes in your life which must last forever and ever.

I cannot finish without introducing you to Jesus Christ as your personal Savior. I invite you to pray:

> *Lord Jesus Christ, I repent of all my sins. I confess that you are my only Savior. I declare with my mouth that Jesus Christ has come to earth as human being for the glory of God. Holy Spirit of God, fill my whole life and help me to pray. In the name of Jesus Christ. Amen.*

> *"For God so loved the world that he gave his one and only Son, that whoever believes in him shall not perish but have eternal life. (John 3:16.*

The Lord bless you and keep you. The Lord make his face shine on you and be gracious to you. The Lord turn his face toward you and give you peace. Shalom.

WHAT MEN MUST KNOW ABOUT WOMEN... A REMINDER

- She needs security and protection.

- She needs to be affirmed and ensured she is the only woman in his life.

- A woman feels really satisfied when she has her own house. Buy a house for her.

- She is your helper, praying for you all the time.

- She likes knowing she is always on your mind, that you choose a beautiful dress for her and imagine her in it, that you like hugging her.

- Don't have secrets in order to avoid anguish and arguments.

- She naturally wishes to please and respect you.

- She is subtle, unpredictable and extraordinary.

- She generally falls in love with a helpful man.

- She feels she is really loved when you listen to her, take care of her and when you walk hand in hand.

- Entrust your credit cards and bank accounts numbers to her.

- Entrust the finances to her, for her to manage.

- Let her see your cell phone.

- Show yourself as a strong and brave man.

- Have a heart of service.

- Sit down at the table with your family. This establishes effective bonds and reinforces the self-esteem of each family member.

- Everyday make her fall in love with you through kind words.

- Pray for your wife outloud, minister to her with God's Word.

- Caress her soul with romantic words

- Find a way to help her lose weight and also care for her body.

- There's nothing better in romance than when you smell good.

- When you introduce her to people, do it proudly: "She is my wife", "She is my girlfriend".

- You have to be the center of attention for her and she for you.

- You must always trust her and she in you.

- Surprise her by inviting her to go out together.

- Help her to make her dreams come true.

- Calm down her anxiety with love and patience.

- Don't give place to anger.

- You must be her confidant because she can talk to you about any topic.

- Work in her self-esteem. Help her to feel she is beautiful and valued through words, gestures, hugs and kisses.

WHAT WOMEN MUST KNOW ABOUT MEN... A REMINDER

- Man responds to a woman's flattery and kindness.

- A true man is generous. He always provides for his wife and children.

- He needs to be reaffirmed and guarantee his power position.

- A faithful man is very much appreciated and highly valued because he is a man of covenant.

- Man is the main provider of his family.

- Man is a natural-born conqueror.

- It is really marvelous to have a good sense of humor and to respect each other.

- Men do not like direct confrontation.

- Man is sensitive to his wife's words of admiration.

- Man always needs to feel that he catches his wife's attention, that he is admired and respected by his wife.

- He yearns to be needed by her.

- Man is also sensitive and needs to be her priority.

- He must enjoy his job.

- He must be determined in all his acts.

ABOUT THE AUTHOR

Apostle Adriana Calabria turns into an author with her first book, "Man's greatest frustration: Not understanding his wife".. She is an international public speaker for women and couples, doctorate minister in Theology and Pastoral Care. Of Italian origin, Argentine nationality and a U.S. citizen. She was raised in the teachings of God's Word since her childhood.

A leader of firm convictions with a realistic vision and knowledgeable of human relationships and marriage, all based on God's Word. Her validity, her sharp vision about the world we live in, translates into an impressive empathy toward people, especially women.

She has been married to Apostle Osvaldo Díaz for 31 years. They have 3 children: Agustín, married to Saraí; Damaris, married to Doménico; and Daniela. They have two young grandchildren that they enjoy enormously: Ethan and Liam.

After a long judicial career, she responds to a full time calling from God, moving to the state of North Carolina, USA, and founding together with her husband, Apostle Osvaldo Díaz, "Celebration Osvaldo Díaz Ministries (CODM)". This is a worldwide religious organization with churches in: Portugal, European Union, Honduras, Central America, Cuba, Nigeria Africa and Mexico; having been consolidated as a model and platform to later establish a Christian University.

The churches are known as:

Churches in USA: CODM USA

Churches in Portugal: CODM Portugal

Churches in Honduras: "Reino de Dios" CODM (Kingdom of God)

Churches in Mexico and Argentina (They are in process of registration).

Nigeria, Africa: Annex of the Christian University of CODM

Adriana Calabria has two passions: to help women all over the world to find their place in the world to serve God and to be a counselor. She and her husband are bearers of a lifestyle that is a testimony to marriages and families.

Adriana Calabria

For presentations, conferences, workshops and
wholesale book purchases, please contact:

Dr. Adriana Calabria
5707 Guess Rd.
Durham, NC 27712

Tel. 01-919-381-4888

AdrianaCalabria.com

www.ingramcontent.com/pod-product-compliance
Lightning Source LLC
LaVergne TN
LVHW052023080426
835513LV00018B/2121